AZTEC

Artist's representation of the palace gardens in Tenochtitlan.

AZTEC

The World of Moctezuma

Jane S. Day

WITH A FOREWORD BY
Eduardo Matos Moctezuma

Denver Museum
of
Natural History
AND
Roberts Rinehart
Publishers

ACKNOWLEDGMENTS

Grupo Financiero Banamex Accival, S.A. de C.V.
(Banacci) and its Boulder-based broker-dealer
subsidiary, ACCI Securities, Inc., generously
contributed to the publication of this book.

This book is published in conjunction with the exhibition,
"AZTEC: The World of Moctezuma," sponsored by the
Blue Cross and Blue Shield Plans of
Colorado, Nevada, and New Mexico.
Exhibition dates at the Denver Museum of Natural History:
September 26, 1992 – February 21, 1993

Editor: Karen M. Nein
Artifact Photography: Michel Zabé, © CNCA–INAH–MEX
Book Design: Ann W. Douden
Manuscript Review: Doris Heyden, National Autonomous
    University of Mexico, Mexico City
Descriptions of Artifacts from the National Museum of
    Anthropology, Mexico City: Felipe Solis Olguin
Descriptions of Artifacts from the Templo Mayor Museum,
    Mexico City: Bertina Olmedo Vera
Exhibition Design: David W. Pachuta

Published in the United States of America by
    Roberts Rinehart Publishers
    Post Office Box 666
    Niwot, Colorado 80544

Published in Great Britain, Ireland, and Europe by
    Roberts Rinehart Publishers
    3 Bayview Terrace, Schull
    West Cork, Republic of Ireland

Published in Canada by
    Key Porter Books
    70 The Esplanade
    Toronto, Ontario M5E 1R2

Library of Congress Catalog Card Number 92-60266
International Standard Book Number 1-879373-19-X

Printed in Hong Kong by Sing Cheong/Colorcorp

*Artist's rendition of the patio of a typical
Aztec house.*

Contents

Artist's interpretation of the Templo Mayor within the sacred precinct of Tenochtitlan.

FOREWORD

EDUARDO MATOS MOCTEZUMA

Director, Templo Mayor Museum,
Mexico City

From the time humans arrived on our continent many thousands of years ago, they have evolved through several levels of development and have left their mark on the land we now call America. Even the earliest humans used the environment for survival. They created stone and wooden tools to hunt, and collected wild plants to satisfy their basic hunger and to provide protection from the cold. The practice of agriculture developed between 5,000 and 7,000 years ago, when humans first domesticated plants such as avocado, corn, beans, squash, and chili peppers. Agriculture eventually became the principal means of sustenance, causing a change from nomadic to sedentary life and new forms of social and economic organization. Religion became increasingly important as elements such as water, the earth, and the sun became deified. In some parts of the continent, this process of development led to the rise of complex societies. As the great cities arose, civilizations became highly stratified, with powerful rulers and nobility controlling all aspects of society—warfare, trade, markets, and religious structure.

Today we can examine the past and become acquainted with one of these groups: the Aztecs. Although the origins of the Aztecs are lost in time, we know they came to the Valley of Mexico from their mythic homeland of Aztlan, the "Place of the Herons." The first years of the Aztecs' long migration were filled with difficulties until they finally arrived in central Mexico. There, on an island in the middle of Lake Texcoco, they founded the city of Tenochtitlan in A.D. 1325. In only two centuries, the Aztecs developed a remarkable culture. Beginning as subjects to other groups, the Aztecs attained their liberation in 1428. During the next 100 years they expanded their territory and took control of a large area of Mesoamerica. Although primarily an agricultural and warrior society, the Aztecs also created magnificent works of art. They were unsurpassed as stone sculptors, ceramicists, and builders. In the masterpieces created by anonymous artists who carved in stone and clay their own concept of the universe, we are provided with a dramatic view of Aztec culture.

While all artists were respected in Aztec culture, painters were of special importance; they created ancient Aztec books called codices. Masters of symbolism and keepers of the tradition, painters were believed to be descendants of the revered, ancient Toltecs. An ancient Aztec song describes the painter, the *tlacuilo*, the one who creates with colors:

> The good painter is a Toltec, an artist;
> he creates with red and black ink,
> . . . .
>
> The good painter is wise,
> God is in his heart.
> He puts divinity into things;
>
> he converses with his own heart.[1]

1. *Moctezuma Xocoyotzin*
oil on canvas
71 ³⁄₅ x 41 ⁹⁄₁₀ inches (182 x 106.5 cm)

Moctezuma Xoyocotzin, the last great Aztec ruler, was 52 years old when the Aztec empire fell. He personified the ideals and beliefs of his culture in his exemplary behavior as well as his physical appearance.

MOCTEZUMA II
1467-1520

2. The glyph of Moctezuma II from the Codex Mendoza *shows the Aztec ruler wearing his traditional blue crown, or diadem.*

Moctezuma II, or Moctezuma Xocoyotzin (the younger), was the last great Aztec ruler. Born in 1467, he grew up as a young nobleman during the most prestigious years of the Aztec empire, when the capital city, Tenochtitlan, was at its height of power. Trained as a priest and warrior, Moctezuma was one of the empire's two highest military commanders when he was chosen emperor in 1502.

From 1502 until his death in 1520, Moctezuma Xocoyotzin was the absolute ruler of the vast and powerful Aztec state. During his reign, he led major military expeditions, put down rebellions, and attempted to confirm and solidify the borders of the empire. He imposed heavy taxes and sumptuary laws upon his subjects.

Moctezuma was described as pious, proud, severe, and implacable but just. The Aztecs regarded him as semidivine. He governed as a mighty warrior, stern father, and the embodiment of the god of kings, Tezcatlipoca. In his physical being, comportment, and accomplishments, Moctezuma was the embodiment of the ideals of his culture. He was a symbol of the wealth, sophistication, and power of the Aztec empire.

The only physical description of Moctezuma is recorded in the words of Bernal Díaz del Castillo, a chronicler and soldier in Cortés's army.

The great [Moctezuma] was about forty years old, of good height, well proportioned, spare and slight, and not very dark. . . . He did not wear his hair long but just over his ears, and he had a short black beard, well-shaped and thin. His face was rather long and cheerful, he had fine eyes, and in his appearance and manner could express geniality or, when necessary, a serious composure. [2]

SOURCES OF INFORMATION

More information about the Aztecs exists than for any other Precolumbian culture of the Americas. Our knowledge of the world of Moctezuma can be traced to specific sources. One source is the Aztec oral tradition that was transcribed into a written form of Nahuatl (the Aztec language) by Spanish friars shortly after the conquest. Another source is the ancient Aztec books called codices. Although Spanish soldiers and priests destroyed most of these codices during the first years following the conquest because they believed them to be symbols of heathen religion, some did survive. Today surviving manuscripts are housed in libraries and archives in Europe and the Americas.

Another source is the reports and impressions of the Spanish soldiers who carefully recorded what they first saw in New Spain. Hernán Cortés himself wrote five long letters to King Charles V, describing the progress and events of the conquest. Fifty years after the fall of the Aztec empire, the Spanish foot soldier Bernal Díaz del Castillo wrote personal recollections of the magnificent Aztec empire and the siege and final battle for Tenochtitlan in 1521.

A third source is the writings of Spanish friars who traveled to Mexico shortly after the conquest. Dedicated friars, such as the Franciscan Bernardino de Sahagún and the Dominican Diego Durán came to Mexico in an effort to convert the indigenous people to Catholicism. These priests quickly learned Nahuatl. From Indian survivors who had lived in Tenochtitlan and witnessed the last days of the empire, the friars compiled detailed accounts of Aztec history, religion, and daily life. Sahagún recorded his data in the 12-volume *General History of the Things of New Spain* (also called the *Florentine Codex*). Durán's observations are detailed in a three-volume set that includes *The History of the Indies of New Spain*.

The archaeological record of the Aztecs is sparser than the written one. Much of Tenochtitlan was either demolished by the final battle between the Aztecs and Spaniards in 1521 or lies buried beneath colonial and modern Mexico City. Recently, however, excavations in the heart of Mexico City have revealed architectural treasures created by the Aztecs. Information from important sites, such as the Templo Mayor and the great marketplace at Tlatelolco, continues to increase our knowledge of the last great empire of Precolumbian Mesoamerica and its magnificent capital city, Tenochtitlan.

> As long as the world will endure,
> the fame and glory of Mexico-Tenochtitlan
> will never perish.[3]

Introduction

3. According to the Codex Boturini, the Aztecs left their island homeland of Aztlan in around A.D. 1000. At Teoculhuacan, the first stop on their migration, their patron god Huitzilopochtli spoke to his people from within a cave. After leaving the mountain, the Aztecs joined other groups of travelers. Guided by four priests who carried an idol of the god, the Aztecs and the other groups continued their journey southward.

Humans have lived and flourished for thousands of years in the clear air and springlike climate of the high central Valley of Mexico. Located at an elevation of over 7,000 feet (2,134 m), the 2,700-square-mile (7,174-sq-km) inland basin is surrounded by a chain of volcanic peaks. In Prehispanic times, streams from the mountains flowed into a series of five shallow, interconnected lakes on the Valley floor, forming a rich habitat for fish, animals, and humans. From the builders of the massive pyramids of Teotihuacan in the first century A.D. to the inhabitants of the vast hub of modern Mexico City, the great Valley has been the heartland of empires.

In the Valley, archaeologists have found remains of mammoth hunters and the great beasts they pursued. They have uncovered the simple homes of early village farmers and have excavated the magnificent cities of the urban-centered warrior-empires that followed.

The mighty Aztecs were the last indigenous group to enter the Valley of Mexico. At their height of power when the Spanish arrived in 1519, they ruled a vast empire from their island capital of Tenochtitlan and created a civilization as sophisticated as any that flourished in Europe at the same time. Like other Precolumbian cultures of Mesoamerica, the Aztecs developed their own unique political system, religion, social structure, agricultural techniques, lifestyle, and world view.

The early Aztecs were seminomadic hunters and farmers. According to legend, in about A.D. 1000 the Aztecs left their mythic, island homeland of Aztlan, the "Place of the Herons," in the desert frontiers of northern Mexico to begin their arduous 200-year migration south to the Valley of Mexico. From Aztlan, the Aztecs traveled to Chicomoztoc, the "Seven Caves," a legendary gathering and departure place for nomadic groups from the north. For at least a thousand years, these groups had been continually moving southward, putting pressure on the great urban states already established in the Valley.

The Aztecs were the last group to leave Seven Caves. Led by their powerful patron god, Huitzilopochtli, they continued their migration southward, stopping along the way, sometimes for several years, to plant crops, to build temples to their god, and to offer human sacrifices in his honor. From groups they encountered as they traveled, the Aztecs adopted new customs and traditions.

When the Aztecs arrived in the Valley of Mexico in about 1193, this fertile inland basin was already heavily populated; little land was available for the travelers from the north. The Aztecs appeared rude and uncivilized to members of the older, more sophisticated city-states that clustered around the Valley's lakes. For another 100 years, while they continued to search for a permanent home, the Aztecs served as mercenary soldiers and servants for their powerful neighbors. They continued to absorb the traditions, manners, and customs of the more advanced and established communities around them.

4. At Tamoanchan, a tree next to a temple dedicated to Huitzilopochtli broke in half—a bad omen for the travelers. Huitzilopochtli instructed the Aztecs to break away from the other groups and continue their migration alone. Along the way, the Aztecs performed sacrifices, including human sacrifices, to honor their god.

5. The Aztecs ended their migration when they found an eagle perched on a nopal cactus—a sign foretold by Huitzilopochtli. In this drawing from the Codex Mendoza, *the city's founders are shown seated around the eagle.*

According to legend, the Aztecs finally settled at a spot where an eagle sat on a nopal cactus—a sign foretold by Huitzilopochtli. The sign finally appeared on a small, rocky island in Lake Texcoco.

> The heart fell onto a stone, and from that heart sprouted a nopal cactus which is now so large and beautiful that an eagle makes his nest [there]. . . . You will find [him] at all hours of the day, and around him you will see scattered many feathers—green, blue, red, yellow, and white. . . . And to this place . . . I give the name Tenochtitlan. [4]

The eagle was the symbol of the sun and Huitzilopochtli himself, god of war and the sun. The red fruit of the nopal cactus represented the hearts offered to the god in human sacrifice. The eagle, with a snake in its mouth, perched on a cactus is the symbol of modern Mexico.

In 1325, on the island, the Aztecs built a temple to Huitzilopochtli and began to construct the city of Tenochtitlan, the "Place of the Prickly Pear Cactus Fruit." Over the next 200 years, the city became one of the largest and most powerful cities of the world, and the heart of the Aztec empire.

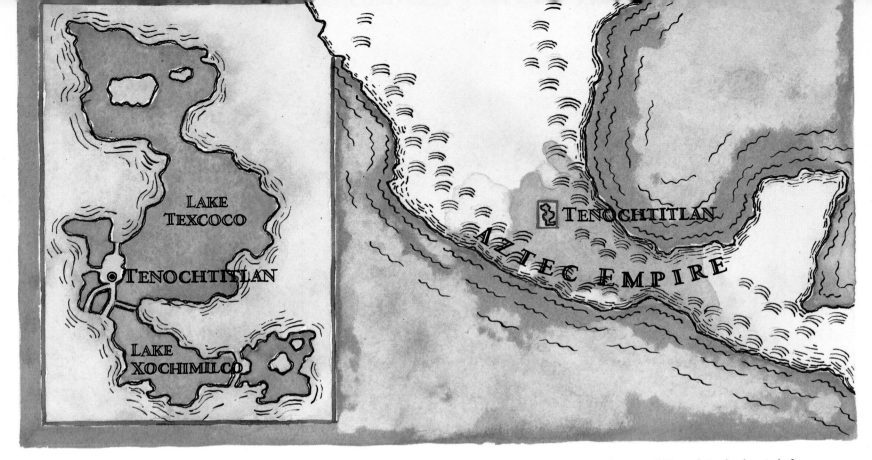

The Aztecs at first were only a small, weak community among the city-states that occupied the Valley. Soon, through political alliances with their neighbors, careful marriages with important families, and ruthless warfare, they began to acquire powerful allies. Their first objective was to gain acceptance and status in the Valley by marrying into the bloodline of the ancient, royal Toltecs. In 1372, a new ruler, Acamapichtli—the son of an Aztec nobleman and a Toltec princess—was selected to rule the fledgling Aztec city-state. All successive Aztec rulers were descended from Acamapichtli's lineage and thus claimed Toltec heritage.

Beginning in 1428, under the leadership of Itzcoatl (Obsidian Snake), the Aztecs created a partnership with the powerful communities of Texcoco and Tlacopan, and formed the Triple Alliance, which waged aggressive wars and eventually established the mighty Aztec empire. Under the guidance of a succession of able rulers, conquests expanded the empire far beyond the Valley of Mexico and provided rich spoils of war from conquered regions. However, the Triple Alliance never conquered the neighboring city-state of Tlaxcalla, to the southeast of Tenochtitlan, nor the mountainous Tarascan region to the north.

6. From their island capital of Tenochtitlan, the Aztecs controlled an empire of 20 million people that reached from coast to coast and south to Guatemala.

The Aztecs eventually assumed the leadership of the Triple Alliance. They commanded the major portion of the militarily enforced tribute paid from vassal states that assured a constant flow of valuable goods such as jade, gold, rubber, food, and slaves into Tenochtitlan. These great riches from throughout the empire supplied Aztec nobility with the wealth to endow their city and themselves with power, culture, and beauty.

The Aztecs were cultural heirs of the past and the final flowering of many ancient Mesoamerican traditions. Three thousand years of experience and knowledge, derived from the Olmec (1500–400 B.C.), Teotihuacan (100 B.C.–A.D. 750), Toltec (A.D. 900–1150), and other cultures, underlay the Aztec empire. Like their predecessors in the Valley of Mexico, the Aztec state maintained a strong urban focus. At the heart of the empire was the magnificent capital city of Tenochtitlan.

Tenochtitlan was built on an island in Lake Texcoco, one of five lakes in the Valley of Mexico. Three causeways connected the island with the mainland; an aqueduct carried fresh water to the city. Edged with beaten dirt pathways, canals with drawbridges formed the city's streets. Thousands of canoes plied the lakes and canals daily, carrying people and materials from place to place. This water traffic was particularly important to a society without the wheel and beasts of burden—a society where the only other means of transportation was by foot. These waterways made transportation and communication efficient, and contributed to the growth and power of Tenochtitlan.

At the heart of the city was a walled sacred precinct dominated by the Templo Mayor, a massive pyramid topped with dual temples dedicated to Tlaloc, the god of rain, and Huitzilopochtli, the god of war and the sun. Temples dedicated to other gods—along with schools for the nobility, living quarters for priests, and a ritual ballcourt—also were located in the precinct. Diego Durán reported that the precinct contained as many as 78 buildings and "must have been immense, for it accommodated eight thousand six hundred men, dancing in a circle."[5]

7. Model of Sacred Precinct of Tenochtitlan
CNCA–INAH–MEX, Museo del Templo Mayor, Mexico City

The sacred precinct was dominated by the Templo Mayor. In front of this massive pyramid was the round temple of Quetzalcoatl, in the guise of Ehecatl, god of the wind.

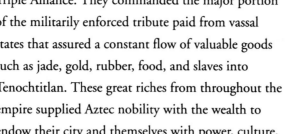

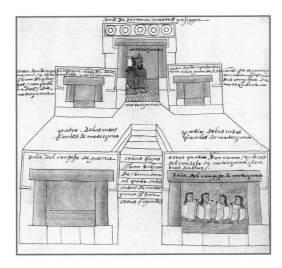

Adjacent to the sacred precinct was the magnificent palace of Moctezuma. The palace was the administrative center for the empire as well as the splendid residence of the ruler. The palace had numerous rooms and apartments, large open courtyards, storage rooms, judicial chambers, servants' quarters, beautiful gardens, an aviary, and a zoo. Administration buildings and houses for the nobility also were concentrated in the central part of the city.

The rest of Tenochtitlan stretched into the lake, covering artificial islands connected by canals and bridges. The city was divided into four quarters, which were further divided into smaller neighborhood units, each called a *calpulli*. The calpulli was the basic social, economic, and political unit of Aztec society. Each calpulli provided the essentials of life for its members: land to farm, markets, temples and priests, schools, and communal support in illness and old age. When called upon, men of a calpulli fought together in war.

In 1519, over 1 million people inhabited the Valley of Mexico. As many as 250,000 people lived in Tenochtitlan. People from all corners of the empire were drawn to this great city. Artists came to employ their skills in the service of the ruler and his nobles. Warriors won fame and fortune in battles of conquest. Traders with their burden-laden human caravans carried exotic treasures to the great marketplace. Foreign dignitaries paid state visits to the court of Moctezuma. People traded for everyday necessities or for luxury items reserved exclusively for the nobility. Citizens listened to the orations of priests, sought the services of soothsayers and healers, dined on their favorite foods prepared at market stalls, and visited with friends. All Aztecs participated in the city's rich ceremonial life that was directed by priests. They watched with awe as human sacrifices were offered to the insatiable gods on the tops of the majestic pyramids. This stimulating and exciting urban center was Tenochtitlan, the heart of the great Aztec empire.

> Proud of itself
> is the city of Mexico-Tenochtitlan.
> Here no one fears to die in war.
> . . . .
> Have this in mind, oh princes,
> do not forget it.
> Who could conquer Tenochtitlan?
> Who could shake the foundation of
>   heaven?[6]

8. *In the* Codex Mendoza, *Moctezuma is shown seated on the second floor of his palace, located near the sacred precinct of Tenochtitlan. He is recognized by his turquoise crown.*

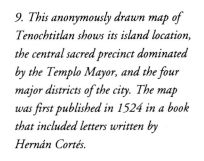

9. *This anonymously drawn map of Tenochtitlan shows its island location, the central sacred precinct dominated by the Templo Mayor, and the four major districts of the city. The map was first published in 1524 in a book that included letters written by Hernán Cortés.*

Aztec society was structured as a social hierarchy with nobles at the top. Social status was determined primarily by birth. All members of the nobility, for example, traced their lineage directly to the first Aztec ruler, Acamapichtli. Except by outstanding military achievement, an individual had little chance to rise within the system.

The populace was divided into two major classes: the nobility and the commoners. Both of the major classes were further divided into different ranks. Some intermediate positions existed between the nobility and the commoners. Luxury artisans called *toltecah* and long-distance traders, the *pochtecah*, held these intermediate ranks. They could accumulate great wealth and often wielded substantial power. They never, however, were considered nobles; they did not have a royal heritage.

Among the nobility were rulers—the *tlatoque*, chiefs—the *tetecutin*, and nobles—the *pipiltin*. The highest ranking ruler was the Aztec emperor, the leader of the Triple Alliance, who governed the mighty Aztec empire. Other tlatoque ruled over smaller cities and towns. The tetecutin controlled smaller areas than rulers and often held high military offices and government positions. The pipiltin, the children of rulers and chiefs, held positions such as tribute collectors, teachers, priests, and bureaucratic officials. Nobles controlled most of the wealth in Aztec society. Their life-styles were different and more luxurious than those of the commoners.

Commoners, free men and women of the society, were called *macehualtin*. They were the backbone of society, forming the large labor and military forces that maintained and protected the empire. As farmers, they grew much of the food that fed the large Aztec population. Macehualtin were born as members of a calpulli.

Two ranks of society existed below the commoners: the *mayeque* and the slaves (*tlacotin*). Mayeque were landless commoners who were not part of a calpulli; they were bound to the land of nobles as serfs. Some slaves were captives taken in war, but often enslavement was punishment for a crime, usually theft, or the result of gambling debts. People also sold themselves or their children into slavery during times of famine or hardship. Slavery, however, was not hereditary and was reversible. Individuals could buy their freedom if their fortune improved.

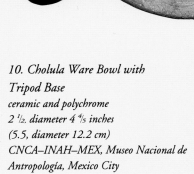

10. *Cholula Ware Bowl with Tripod Base*
ceramic and polychrome
2 ¹/₂ diameter 4 ⁴/₅ inches
(5.5, diameter 12.2 cm)
CNCA–INAH–MEX, Museo Nacional de Antropología, Mexico City

11. Overview of Tenochtitlan
pastel on paper
36 x 81 inches (91 x 206 cm)

In November 1519, the Spanish Captain Hernán Cortés, his soldiers, and many Indian allies wound down a high mountain pass into the verdant Valley of Mexico. From across the lake, the Spaniards had their first view of Tenochtitlan. The seasoned Spanish soldiers who accompanied Cortés were overwhelmed by the beauty and size of the city. Built of stone, adobe, and wood, the city with its whitewashed stucco walls shone in the sun like silver. Thousands of canoes floated on the lake and traveled along the city's canals. The soldiers gazed in wonder at the gardens, palaces, temples, and pyramids that seemed to rise from the water.

Bernal Díaz recorded his impression of the mighty Aztec capital.

> And when we saw all those cities and villages built in the water, and other great towns on dry land, and that straight and level causeway leading to Mexico, we were astounded. These great towns and cues [temples] and buildings rising from the water, all made of stone, seemed like an enchanted vision. . . . Indeed, some of our soldiers asked whether it was not all a dream. . . . It was all so wonderful . . . this first glimpse of things never heard of, seen or dreamed before.[7]

The Chinampa System:
How the Empire Was Fed

Tenochtitlan was a city of lake dwellers. Nowhere was this more apparent than in the drained field system of the farmers, who formed the backbone of Aztec society. These free men and women farmed, crafted the utensils of daily life, cooked the meals, maintained the city's buildings and canals, fought in wars, and paid tribute in goods and labor to the noble families of the city.

Many farmers lived on the outskirts of the great city on fabricated rectangular plots of land called *chinampas*, which measured about 300 feet (100 m) by 30 feet (9 m). Chinampas, the basic agricultural units of the Valley of Mexico, were part of one of the most intensive

systems of agriculture ever developed. Through careful cultivation and cycling of crops, farmers provided food for the thriving Aztec capital. As the empire expanded and the population increased, requiring additional food to survive, more and more of these islands were created for cultivation.

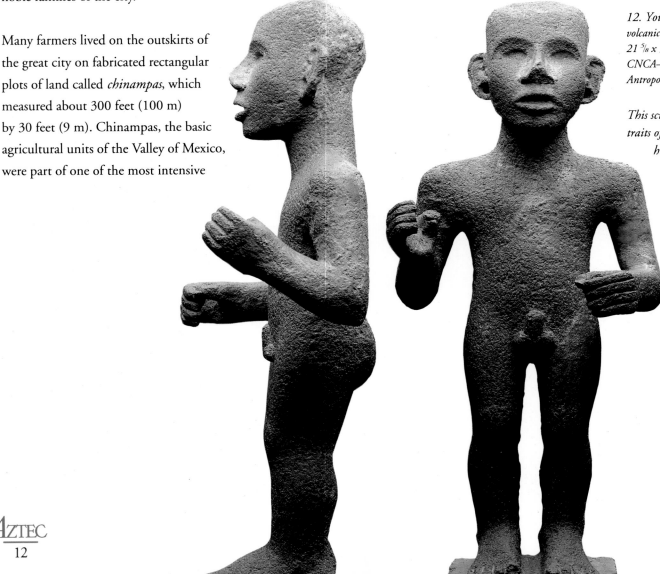

12. Young Macehualli
volcanic stone
21 ⁵/₈ x 7 ⁷/₈ x 5 ⁷/₈ inches (55 x 20 x 15 cm)
CNCA–INAH–MEX, Museo Nacional de Antropología, Mexico City

This sculpture shows some of the physical traits of the Aztec people: wide-set eyes, high foreheads, prominent cheekbones, and broad noses. They had straight black hair, dark eyes, and light brown skin. Women stood about 4 feet 10 inches (148 cm) tall; men averaged about 5 feet 3 inches (160 cm).

13. A small area of the original chinampas can be seen at Xochimilco in modern Mexico City.

Chinampa fields were reclaimed from the swampy areas around the lakes by cutting drainage canals through the marshes. Between the canals, plots were staked off with poles lashed together with vines and filled with alternating layers of rotting aquatic plants and fertile mud from the lake bed. Layers were added until the island was higher than the water level. Willow trees *(Salix bonplandiana)* were planted at each corner and along the sides of each plot. Their rapidly growing roots anchored the plot to the lake bottom and reduced erosion. Chinampas were fertilized with human waste collected from public latrine boats in the city and fertile soil from the lake bottom.

Farmers germinated seedlings in small beds and then transplanted them into larger fields as other crops were harvested and space became available. With this efficient system of crop production and water from the canals readily available, farmers harvested as many as seven crops a year. Much of the produce was used to pay tribute to the state or to the nobility. The remaining food was eaten by farming families or exchanged at the local market.

14. Today in Mexico City, farmers still grow corn on chinampas.

15. Cut-away Model of Chinampa Construction
CNCA–INAH–MEX, Museo del Templo Mayor, Mexico City

On the chinampas Aztec farmers grew the foods native to the Prehispanic Americas. Corn, beans, and squash were the principal crops in Tenochtitlan, just as they are throughout Mexico today. Corn, the main staple of life, was grown in many varieties, sizes, and colors. Corn was eaten in many ways: as a gruel called *atolli*, as flattened cakes called tortillas, and as tamales—cornmeal filled with various ingredients and steamed inside cornhusks. Tamales, a favorite food of the Aztecs, were served at special occasions and prepared in many different ways.

> White tamales with beans forming a sea shell on top;
>
> white tamales with maize grains thrown in . . .
>
> red tamales with beans forming a sea shell on top;
>
> . . . . . .
>
> Tamales made of maize flowers with ground amaranth seed and cherries added . . .
>
> tamales made with honey.[8]

A mystical relationship existed between the Aztecs and corn. Corn was honored in all its various forms—as seeds, as tender young plants, and as mature plants. Several deities were associated with corn, among them Centeotl the young male god of tender maize, and Chicomecoatl, goddess of our sustenance. When women put maize in an olla

> first of all they breathed upon it . . . [so it] would not take fright . . . it would not fear the heat.
>
> . . . .
>
> if [women] saw or came upon dried grains of maize lying scattered on the ground, then they quickly gathered them up. They said: "Our sustenance suffereth: it lieth weeping. If we should not gather it up, it would accuse us before our lord."[9]

Aztec farmers also grew fruits of many kinds, as well as tomatoes, avocados, chili peppers from mild to very hot, herbs, and gourds. Chiles were the basic seasoning for foods. They were so vital for flavor that during periods of penance and fasting, common in Aztec ritual life, food was not seasoned with chili peppers or salt.

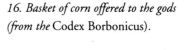

16. Basket of corn offered to the gods (*from the* Codex Borbonicus).

17. Aztec farmers, hardworking and frugal, stored harvested corn and other grains in pottery storage jars and baskets (*from the* Florentine Codex).

18. Chicomecoatl, Goddess of Our Sustenance
stone with red pigment
9 x 5 ½ inches (23 x 14 cm)
CNCA–INAH–MEX, Museo Nacional de Antropología, Mexico City

Chicomecoatl, also known as the goddess of mature corn, is adorned with her characteristic paper headdress. In her right hand she carries a rattle staff; in her left are two ears of corn.

19. Macehualtin who farmed the chinampas used simple wooden tools to plant and cultivate their crops. Ripened corn, carefully harvested by hand, fed the family and was used to pay taxes to the state. Any excess food grown by the diligent farmer was traded at market (from the Florentine Codex).

Many flowers also were grown on the chinampas. The Aztecs loved flowers, which they used in religious rituals, as decorations for costumes, and in temples. They were made into bouquets to be carried around and enjoyed for their beauty and aroma.

Aztec farmers and their families lived in mud-walled, thatch-roofed huts on chinampa plots. These small houses usually consisted of one room with a dirt floor, covered with woven reed mats used for sleeping and sitting. The farming family rose with the sun to begin work. The day ended when darkness fell. At mid-morning, the family ate a simple meal—usually corn gruel. The main, midday meal normally consisted of tortillas and beans, made savory with chiles and salt, and occasionally tamales.

Many activities of daily life took place outside in the carefully swept dooryards of the simple homes. Women and girls wove cloth on backstrap looms and prepared the family's meals. They ground corn that had been softened in lime water on a stone *metlatl* and baked tortillas on a flat, round griddle called a *comitl.* The comitl was always placed over the fire on three hearthstones that represented the symbolic heart of every Aztec home.

Men and boys tended their fields and planted crops, using a simple pointed stick called a *huictli.* Meat was in short supply. Farmers raised turkeys, ducks, and small, hairless dogs, which were reserved for the wealthy. The only meat most families ate was collected from nearby lakes: fish, ducks, geese, turtles, frogs, mollusks, crustaceans, insects, grubs, and salamanders. The lakes also provided the Aztecs with an unusual source of protein. Green lake scum that tasted like cheese was dried into bricks called *tecuitlatl*. This high-protein food often was carried by warriors into battle. Some farmers also tended beehives on their chinampa plots. Honey was one of the few sweeteners known in Precolumbian America.

After taxes were paid, any excess food the farmer grew or hunted was loaded onto a canoe and taken to the market. There it was exchanged for other products needed by the farmer and his family.

Farmers did not own the land they cultivated; it belonged to their calpulli. The head of the calpulli kept very careful maps of the calpulli's landholdings. Families were allotted the land they needed from the communal holdings. As families increased or decreased in size, land needs changed. If the family died out, the land returned to the common pool. Because they were part of a communal association, calpulli members worked the fields for those who could not. A calpulli thus provided a form of social security for its members.

Times were not always easy for the farmers. Major famines were remembered with dread. But in the calpulli system, farming families could count on a plot of land to work for their lifetime and a place to live in a well-organized, structured society.

20. In this drawing from the Codex Borbonicus, *Chalchiuhtlicue*, *"she of the jade skirt,"* is shown wearing a headdress and ornaments of paper painted blue and white. The blue and white band around her head and the long tassles that hang on each side of her face also are visible in the statue of the goddess shown below.

21. Chalchiuhtlicue, Goddess of Water
stone
33 $^7/_{10}$ x 16 $^1/_{10}$ inches (85.5 x 41 cm)
CNCA–INAH–MEX, Museo Nacional de Antropología, Mexico City

Chalchiuhtlicue, goddess of rivers, creeks, lakes, and the sea, was a companion of the rain god, Tlaloc. In this sculpture, she is shown as a mature woman who carries a bowl of water in her hands. She wears a headdress of twisted cotton ribbons; two tassles of the same material fall on the sides of her face.

Aztec farmers lived close to nature. They depended on the seasons and natural forces for the success of their crops. As a result, many religious rituals centered around the deities of fertility and water who assured the productivity of their fields. The cult of Tlaloc, the god of rain, was already ancient in the Valley of Mexico when the Aztecs first arrived. Tlaloc and his consort, Chalchiuhtlicue, the goddess of water, were intimately related to the basic needs of farmers in the dry plateau of central Mexico.

The heat of the sun was predictable and constant, but the rains often were capricious. At the end of the dry season, as spring approached, prayers and special offerings were presented to Tlaloc. Through songs, dances, and rituals, the farmers implored him to send down the rains so the new crops could grow. Infants and small children were considered the most appropriate human sacrifice to Tlaloc—their tears symbolized the falling rain. They were sacrificed on the mountaintops where rain clouds were born or in the whirlpools of the lakes. The children's innocence made them especially valuable as messengers to the god of rain.

> The god of the maize is born
> In the garden of rain and mist,
> There where the children of men are
>   made,
> There where they fish for jade fishes.[10]

22. Tlaloc, as shown in the Codex Borbonicus, *wears his characteristic goggle mask and clothing symbolically painted blue, the color of water. His body is painted black, representing storm clouds. White clouds are symbolized by his white heron-feather headdress.*

23. Tlaloc, God of Rain
stone
39 ²/₅ x 14 ³/₅ inches (100 x 37 cm)
CNCA–INAH–MEX, Museo Nacional de Antropología, Mexico City

In this statue, Tlaloc wears a simple loincloth, an elaborate feather headdress, and a mask that appears as wide rings around his eyes. The pleated paper fan at the back of his neck signifies the nobility and importance of this deity.

Life on the City Streets

Although farming was the lifeblood of the Aztec empire, many macehualtin lived in Tenochtitlan and had specialized jobs. Like farmers, city dwellers also were born into a calpulli. These related groups lived together in neighborhoods and often shared a specialized craft and a patron deity. Neighborhood workshops and home industries produced baskets, pottery vessels and figurines, obsidian tools, gourd bowls, reed mats, and great quantities of woven cloth. As in farming communities, much of this production was designated for taxes or family consumption, but some was transported by canoe to be traded at the marketplace.

As a neighborhood unit, the calpulli also provided work crews for city projects and trained warriors who fought together in battle. Each calpulli had its own military officers, elders' council, schools, and local priests and temples.

The one-story homes of the urban macehualtin were made up of several rooms arranged in an **L**-shape around an open patio. Like houses in Mexico today, a

24. Artist's Study of Life on the Streets of Tenochtitlan
pastel on paper
36 x 44 inches (18 x 85 cm)

25. Black and Orange Ware Bowl
ceramic, 3 9/10, diameter 2 1/2 inches
(10.5, diameter 31.7 cm)
CNCA–INAH–MEX, Museo Nacional de
Antropología, Mexico City

Throughout the Valley of Mexico during
the fifteenth and sixteenth centuries,
potters made ceramic bowls, plates, and
other vessels from vibrant orange clay.
They painted the highly polished pieces
with geometric designs.

blank wall for privacy faced the street. The houses,
which bordered the footpaths of the city, often had
adjacent small, chinampa gardens next to the canals.

A house was occupied by an extended family, made
up of parents, children, and grandparents. Family
activities often took place in the patio: meals were
cooked, children played, and neighbors stopped in to
chat and exchange local news.

26. Household Deity with Mold
ceramic mold: 7 7/10 x 4 2/5 x 2 2/5 inches
(19.6 x 11.2 x 6.2 cm)
figure: 6 7/8 x 2 1/2 inches (17.8 x 6.4 cm)
CNCA–INAH–MEX, Museo Nacional de
Antropología, Mexico City

Aztec potters made ceramic figurines in
small detailed molds. The figurines were
made in halves and then glued together.

Some special craftsmen, the toltecah, produced luxury items, such as gold and greenstone jewelry and brilliantly colored feather shields, fans, and capes for the exclusive use of the nobility. These crafters of specialized luxury items were of a higher social class than other craftsmen. They lived together in their own calpulli. Toltecah were organized in a hereditary craft system that, like the guilds of medieval Europe, had apprentices, levels of expertise, and master craftsmen. As artisans, the toltecah were considered heirs of the highly respected, ancient Toltec artists who the Aztec believed invented arts, such as goldsmithing and featherwork. The Aztecs said of the Toltecs:

> The Toltecs, the people of Quetzalcoatl,
> were very skillful.

> Nothing was difficult for them to do.
> They cut precious stones,
> wrought gold,
> and made many works of art
> and marvelous ornaments of feathers.
> Truly they were skillful.[11]

27. Aztec featherworkers, as shown in the Florentine Codex, *crafted colorful shields, headdresses, capes, and banners of exotic feathers using only simple tools.*

28. Tzapotlatena, Goddess of Women Dedicated to Medicine
stone
34 ⅕ x 12 ⅕ inches (87 x 31 cm)
CNCA–INAH–MEX, Museo Nacional de Antropología, Mexico City

Spots of rubber, resin, and tar decorate the cheeks of Tzapotlatena, one of the many Aztec deities associated with medicine and healing. She wears a simple skirt and a rattlesnake belt. Her triangular blouse, called quechquemitl, *is decorated with balls of cotton. The large headdress is decorated with a band of feathers that surrounds the head.*

29. Quachtlacalhuaztli, *an herb used to treat wounds on the scalp, also was used to aid digestion (from the* Florentine Codex).

30. The roots of the medicinal herb, Iztac palancapatli, *were ground and made into a tea, or powdered and applied to heal wounds on the scalp (from the* Florentine Codex).

used massage and steambaths to treat illness and followed the army into battle to treat injured warriors. The good doctor was described by Sahagún:

a diagnostician . . . a knower of herbs, of stones, of trees, of roots. . . . He provides health, restores people, provides them splints, sets bones for them, purges them . . . gives them potions; he lances, he makes incisions in them, stitches them, revives them.[12]

Among the Aztecs, as in much of the world during the sixteenth century, ideas about illness and medicine were a blend of religion, magic, and science. Specific deities were believed to cause certain illnesses or to cure them. Illness often was attributed to black magic and could be healed only by sorcery and divination.

Yet some Aztec medicine was quite scientific. Healers and physicians used as many as 132 medicinal herbs and plants as emetics, diuretics, sedatives, and purges. Physicians, called *ticitl,* also

THE LIFE CYCLE

In Aztec society, everyone had a well-defined place and followed strict rules of behavior that stressed honesty, modesty, obedience, and moderation. From infancy, an individual's roles and responsibilities were clearly laid out.

Children were much desired, a gift from the gods. They were brought into the world by a midwife who cut the umbilical cord. If the baby was a girl, the cord was buried at the hearth to symbolize her life dedicated to the home. If the baby was a boy, the midwife left the cut umbilical cord to dry. It later was buried by a warrior of the calpulli on the battlefield, dedicating the boy's life to warfare. The midwife bathed the baby and welcomed him or her with words of affection and warnings about the nature of the world.

"Precious necklace, precious feather, precious green stone, precious bracelet, precious turquoise, thou wert created in the place of duality . . . Thou hast come to reach the earth, the place of torment, the place of pain, where it is hot, where it is cold . . . It is the place of one's affliction, of one's weariness, a place of thirst, a place of hunger . . . a place of weeping."13

Once the baby was welcomed into the family by kin and neighbors, an astrologer selected a propitious day for the naming ceremony. If the child had been born on a lucky day, the naming took place immediately.

If the birth day was unlucky, the naming ceremony was postponed for up to four days until the next lucky day on the ritual calendar. After the child was given a name, small boys ran through the neighborhood streets, announcing the baby's name at every door.

A banquet followed, during which guests were garlanded with flowers and given pipes of tobacco to smoke. Indeed, feasts and ceremonies were part of the celebration of all of life's moments of passage. Their degree of elaboration depended only upon the means of the family. Among noble and wealthy families, the celebration was rich with food and gifts. Celebrations of the poor were more modest.

31. Before the baby was named, the midwife gave the newborn gifts. A boy received a small shield and a miniature bow and four arrows—the weapons of a warrior whose mission was to feed the sun with the blood of captives taken in battle. A baby girl was given miniature weaving tools—symbols of her future duties as a wife and mother (from the Codex Mendoza).

32. By the time a girl was 13, she knew how to grind softened corn on a stone metlatl, and helped prepare the family's meals (from the Codex Mendoza).

33. By age 14, a young man knew how to fish (from the Codex Mendoza).

34. At age 11, boys and girls were punished by being held over the acrid smoke of a fire in which red chili peppers were burning (from the Codex Mendoza).

Throughout childhood, girls and boys were taught their responsibilities by their mothers and fathers. From an early age, mothers taught daughters how to spin thread on a spindle, how to weave cloth on a backstrap loom, how to grind softened corn kernels on a stone metlatl and help in the preparation of the family's meal. All women in Aztec society—noblewomen and commoners alike—were expected to be accomplished weavers.

From an early age, fathers taught their sons to carry water and firewood, to collect and bring home whatever marketgoers dropped or left behind at the local market, and how to fish with a net from a canoe.

All children were expected to conform to the structured Aztec society and to work and contribute to the needs of the household.

The idle or disobedient child was severely punished. In addition, parents and elders were constantly giving orations and good advice on proper conduct and the ideal Aztec life of conformity and moderation.

From age 12 to about 15, both boys and girls attended the local temple school, the *cuicacalli*, or "house of song," where they learned the songs and dances that were part of the yearly cycle of elaborate Aztec rituals. Boys continued their formal education beginning at age 15. They attended either the *calmecac* (reserved for youth from the nobility) or the *telpochcalli*, "the young men's house," reserved for commoners. At the telpochcalli, until about age 20, young men were trained as warriors and performed physical labor such as building walls and digging canals.

Girls were married at 15, boys at about age 20. When a young man was ready for marriage, his parents consulted matchmakers who approached the prospective bride's parents to set the dowry and make final arrangements. Soothsayers and astronomers then picked an auspicious day for the wedding.

An elaborate wedding feast was planned at the bride's home for the day before the marriage.

> Ground cacao was prepared, flowers were secured . . . tubes of tobacco were prepared, sauce bowls and pottery cups and baskets were purchased. Then maize was ground. . . . Then tamales were prepared . . . perhaps three days . . . the women made tamales.[14]

Families and friends came and went all day, bearing gifts and eating and drinking. Toward sunset, the bride was dressed and her face was decorated with red feathers and dye. Old men of the groom's family spoke to the new bride:

> "Forever now leave childishness, girlishness; no longer art thou to be like a child . . . Be most considerate . . . regard one with respect, speak well . . . By night look to . . . the sweeping, the laying of the fire. . . . Do not embarrass us."[15]

At the groom's home, the bride was seated on a mat in front of the hearth. There the groom's cape was symbolically tied to her shift.

With marriage bonds established, the young husband and wife assumed adult responsibilities. If they survived illness, childbirth, warfare, and death by

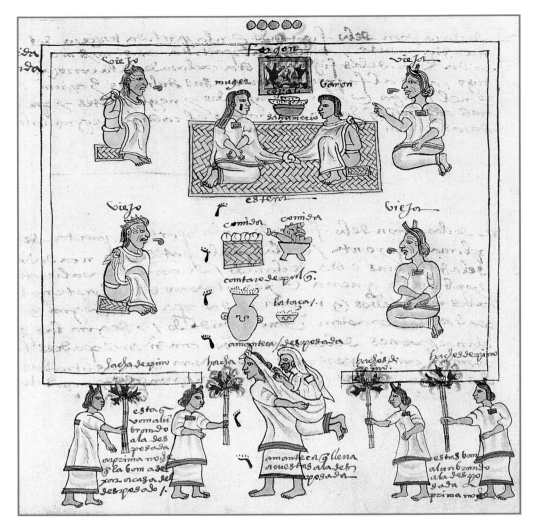

sacrifice, they lived to old age—a time that held special privileges for the Aztecs. Elders were treated with respect and played important roles in ceremonies. Their long, rambling speeches of advice to their young relatives were tolerated, if not encouraged.

Above all, old people were allowed to drink alcoholic beverages to excess. They alone could become intoxicated without fear of punishment; no one else in society was supposed to become drunk. The many

35. Female members of the groom's family carried the bride to her new home in a torchlit musical procession through the city's streets (from the Codex Mendoza).

36. Old men and women over age 70 were served the alcoholic beverage pulque *by their grandchildren (from the* Codex Mendoza*)*.

laws and exhortations against public drunkenness suggest major drinking problems within Aztec society. In fact, the death sentence was enforced for nobles who appeared drunk in public; lesser penalties threatened commoners.

After death, most people were cremated and sent to the afterlife with a sacrificed dog as a guide and a bead in their mouths symbolizing the soul. In the Aztec world, a person's destination after death depended not on how he or she had lived life on earth, but on how he or she had died. After death, most people wandered for four years, finally ending up in Mictlan, the "Place of Darkness," the "Place of No Return." Only a fortunate few could look forward to something better. Among the lucky ones were people who died by drowning. They went to Tlalocan, the watery, green region of the rain god Tlaloc, where water was plentiful, food was abundant, and life was pleasant. Small children went to Chichihuacuauhco "Place of the Wet-nurse Tree," which was located in the house of Tonacatecuhtli (Lord of our Flesh).

Some of the most beautiful Aztec poetry concerned death. Most Aztecs saw their demise as a final and irrevocable end to life. Poems expressed a dark, fatalistic view that saw life on earth as transient, with the darkness and cold of the grave its only reward:

> I am come, oh my friends,
> with necklaces I entwine you,
>
> . . . .
>
> I embrace mankind.
> With trembling quetzal feathers,
> with circlets of song,
>
> . . . .
>
> I will carry you with me to the palace
> where we all,
> someday,
> all must betake ourselves,
> to the region of the dead.
> Our life has only been loaned to us![16]

The Great Marketplace:
Economic Center of the Empire

Markets were the heart and pulse of Aztec daily life. They flourished in urban centers and villages throughout the empire and in the many neighborhoods of Tenochtitlan. The greatest market of all was held daily at Tlatelolco. There, in the great plaza, a wooden drum sounded from the top of the temple of Quetzalcoatl at morning and evening to announce the beginning and end of the market day.

When the Spanish arrived in 1519, Tlatelolco was part of Tenochtitlan. Before 1473, however, it was a separate Aztec city, located on the lake only about 1 mile (1.6 m) from the capital itself. Established by Aztec-related people at about the same time as Tenochtitlan, Tlatelolco became a vital trading center with great commercial wealth. As it grew rich and powerful, the rulers of Tenochtitlan began to view this city as a threat to their own authority. The Aztec emperor Axayacatl forcibly incorporated Tlatelolco into Tenochtitlan. Once defeated, Tlatelolco's independent dynasty was destroyed; its ruler was thrown to his death from the top of the Great Temple of Tlateloco. Thereafter, Tlatelolco was ruled by an officially appointed Aztec military governor. This incorporation placed the focus of both commercial and military might firmly in the hands of Tenochtitlan's ruling elite.

The great marketplace in the central plaza of Tlatelolco continued as the economic center of the Aztec world. Riches such as feathers, gold, and jade from far-flung frontiers of the empire were available for purchase. Locally produced agricultural crops and manufactured products were bartered daily. Shoppers strolled through colorful rows of fruits, flowers, and vegetables; listened to merchants hawking their wares; and enjoyed a snack amid the colorful displays. This immense Aztec market served as many as 25,000 people each day. Its merchandise and activities were strictly controlled by the state. All products sold at the marketplace were subject to taxes; selling or buying outside the market was prohibited by law. In addition, the market maintained its own judges, who settled disputes and administered quick justice.

37. Detail of Tlatelolco market.

38. Detail of Tlatelolco market.

The Spanish were amazed at the market's size, organization, and rich diversity. Bernal Díaz described the great Tlatelolco market:

> We stood there looking . . . [at] the great market and the swarm of people buying and selling. The . . . murmur of their voices talking was loud enough to be heard more than three miles away. Some of our soldiers who had been . . . in Constantinople, in Rome, and all over Italy, said that they had never seen a market so well laid out, so large, so orderly, and so full of people.[17]

39. The great Aztec market at Tlatelolco accommodated as many as 25,000 people each day and offered a wide variety of goods and services.

Díaz also mentioned merchants selling gold, silver, precious stones, male and female slaves, clothing, building materials, food of all kinds, games, pottery, firewood, torches, paper, indigo, flint and obsidian knives, tools, flowers, and precious featherwork.

40. Detail of Tlatelolco market.

Services also were available—barbers, fortune tellers, scribes, and prostitutes were all part of the market scene. The market was a busy and festive place where people gathered to exchange news as well as goods and to meet with friends.

Not all items for sale were of equal value. Although barter of one object or service for another was the basis of Aztec trade, certain items had a standardized worth that allowed unequal exchanges to be conducted. Cacao (chocolate) beans, cotton cloaks, stylized copper knives, and turkey quills filled with gold dust were used to make up differences in the values between objects.

Food and objects used for daily life were provided by local producers and vendors. Expensive luxury items from distant places were brought to the market by professional long-distance merchants called pochtecah. The pochtecah, a hereditary group within Aztec society, lived in special neighborhoods in Tlatelolco and had their own customs, gods, and ceremonies. They also maintained their own courts and judges outside the regular legal system.

As a group, the pochtecah were of particular value to the Aztec elite. The pochtecah carried to Tenochtitlan the luxury items that were reserved exclusively for use by the upper classes of society. They brought to market the jade, silver, precious stones, colorful feathers, gold, jaguar skins, amber, clothing, and chocolate that were the status symbols and prerogatives of the wealthy nobility. Pochtecah maintained "ports of trade" along routes to the south where the precious items originated. These ports were special exchange centers where the constant, ongoing warfare of the Aztec world was not allowed to interrupt the important business of commerce. As these merchants increased the wealth of the ruler and his nobles by their trading expeditions, their own wealth also increased. The growing wealth and power of the pochtecah alarmed the nobility. During the reign of Moctezuma II, the Aztec caste system tightened to exclude from privilege all those not of noble blood, including the pochtecah.

These tightly knit hereditary merchant guilds directed the steady flow of valuable imports and exports to and from Tenochtitlan. They used human caravans of bearers to carry exotic raw materials into the production centers of the capital and to disperse manufactured items from the city's workshops along trade routes. Some of these bearers were slaves; others were free men who hired themselves out as specialized porters, or *tlameme*. They carried loads weighing up to 50 pounds (23 kg) for a distance of about 18 miles (29 m) each day. In addition, they carried war supplies to battle and were hired to carry individuals of high status in litters or hammocks.

The long-distance trade system was the lifeblood of the Aztec empire. Along its routes flowed exotic items for the market and also the Aztec culture, its Nahuatl language, art styles, and deities. Because of trading, distant corners of the empire felt the influence of the Aztec state. This system of long-distance trade often helped open the door to military conquests. The pochtecah sometimes served the emperor as spies, carrying back to Tenochtitlan valuable information about supplies and defenses.

Seeking to extend the borders and the wealth of the empire, the powerful Aztec armies turned trading partners into vassal states. Through conquest, prized objects of trade became militarily enforced tribute, bringing additional riches and captives for ritual sacrifice into Tenochtitlan.

Aztec scribes kept very careful accounts of the tribute owed to the emperor. Some of these colorful pictorial lists are found in the ancient Aztec manuscript, the *Codex Mendoza*. The brightly painted pages contain the actual amounts and types of goods owed by each tribute-paying region, carefully recorded opposite the name glyph for the city-state. Among the highly valued items carried into Tenochtitlan by canoes and human caravans were feathers from the tropics, elaborate eagle and jaguar costumes, thousands of pieces of cotton cloth both plain and heavily embroidered, chocolate in bean and powder form, rubber balls from the Gulf Coast, slaves and honey from the Yucatan, gold and jade from Central America, and food from many regions. The diverse tribute was meticulously inventoried and stored in central warehouses under the supervision of special officials who were accountable to the emperor. The tremendous wealth of the ruling classes and the strength of the empire were dependent upon this combined flow of trade goods and heavy tribute demanded by the Aztecs from conquered city-states.

41. Pochtecah traveled on foot in caravans throughout the empire and beyond, often into hostile lands (from the Florentine Codex).

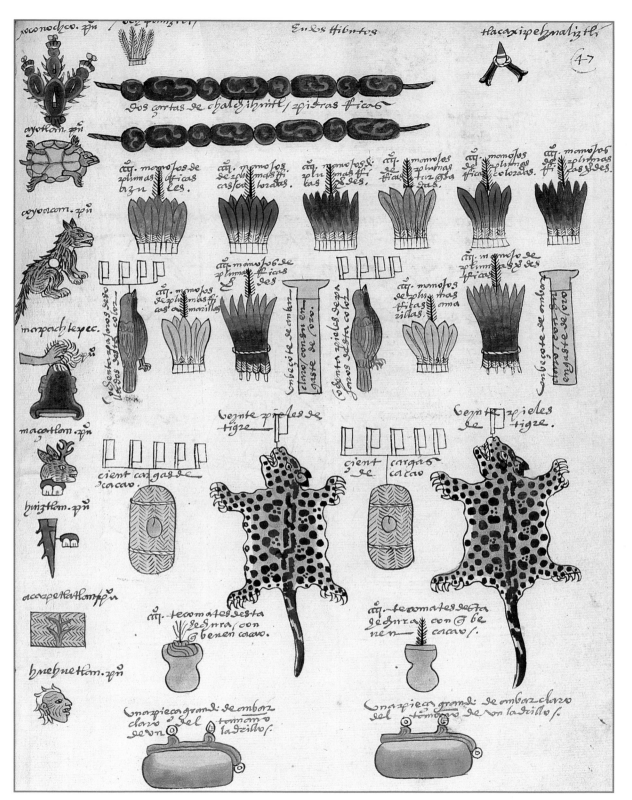

42. This example of a tribute list from the Codex Mendoza, *shows payment of tribute that included 2 strings of green stones, 400 handfuls of blue feathers, 400 handfuls of green feathers, 20 jaguar skins, and 100 loads of cacao.*

The Nobility and Rulers of Tenochtitlan

Within Aztec society, the basic class distinction was between nobles and commoners, who were different in almost all aspects of their lives. Nobles and commoners had very different standards of living, rules of behavior, privileges, and occupations. Nobles controlled most of the wealth in society but paid no taxes. They owned land and controlled the lives of the people who worked for them. Their duties included governing the empire, warfare, religious activities, and bureaucratic responsibilities. Nobles lived in luxurious homes; wore fine clothing and jewels; and enjoyed banquets, music, and games of chance. Noblemen were allowed to have as many wives and concubines as they could support. As a result, their extended families often were very large. Moctezuma, the highest ranking noble in Tenochtitlan, reportedly had 150 children.

Even within the noble class, a strict hierarchy existed—not all were equal. The highest ranking noble was the Aztec emperor, the ruler of the Triple Alliance. Sahagún describes the ideal ruler as

> A protector; one who carries [his subjects] in his arms, who unites them, who brings them together. He rules, takes responsibilities, assumes burdens. . . . He governs; he is obeyed. [To him] as shelter, as refuge, there is recourse.[18]

Always chosen from one lineage, or family, the ruler often was the brother of the preceding ruler, although sons and nephews also could succeed to the throne. This process of an "election" of the ruler by his peers probably had its roots in early Aztec egalitarian society. But even in the last years of the empire, this process helped to ensure that the most able man was elevated to the highest office.

By 1502, when Moctezuma II ascended the Aztec throne, the chieftain of the early migration period had been transformed into a semidivine king. Moctezuma II—son, grandson, and nephew of kings—was 34 years old when he was chosen as emperor. He was carefully selected from a group of royal princes by an electoral body composed of various rulers of the empire and a council of Aztec nobility. The choice was based on Moctezuma's ability as a military commander and on his mature and temperate nature. As ruler, or *tlatoani* (he who speaks), Moctezuma had religious and social duties. But above all, he was commander in chief of the armies; his primary responsibilities were warfare and conquest.

43. Moctezuma and his war array (from the Florentine Codex).

44. In this drawing from the Codex Borbonicus, *Quetzalcoatl, as the god of the wind Ehecatl, wears a conical jaguar cap and a shell-shaped breast plate. His body is painted black; he wears a red beak-shaped mask. He carries the incense bag of a priest in one hand and a serpent in the other.*

The Aztecs prided themselves on their descent from the ancient Toltec kings. During their first difficult years in the Valley of Mexico, the Aztecs joined the blood of their own noble lineage with that of the Toltecs through marriages into the royal house of Quetzalcoatl. The Aztecs came to regard themselves as direct descendants of the god-king who had once ruled at Tula.

The Toltecs were truly wise;
they conversed with their own hearts. . . .
They played their drums and rattles;
they were singers, they composed songs
and sang them among the people;
they guarded the songs in their
memories.[19]

The story of the golden age of the Toltecs under the wise rule of the god-king, Quetzalcoatl, and of how it came to an end when he was tricked into drunkenness and incest by Tezcatlipoca, the ancient dark shaman, was recorded in Aztec literature. Forced to flee from Tula, Quetzalcoatl and his loyal followers went to the Gulf Coast where

They say that in the year I-Reed
. . . .
Quetzalcoatl sacrificed himself
. . . .
When the pyre had ceased to burn,
Quetzalcoatl's heart came forth,
went up to heaven, and entered there.
And the ancient ones say
it was converted to the morning star.[20]

Quetzalcoatl's birth and death both fell in the year *ce acatl* (One Reed) in the Aztec calendar. This date haunted the Aztecs; the Spanish Captain Hernán Cortés landed in Mexico on that same date many years later.

As emperor and acknowledged descendant of Quetzalcoatl, Moctezuma carried the idea of semidivine leadership and nobility to a new height. He insisted that only those of pure noble blood, descended on both sides from the Toltec line, could serve him. Even great lords had to approach him barefoot; no one could look directly into his face. He strictly enforced the sumptuary laws governing personal behavior. These laws dictated what kinds of houses people lived in and what sandals, ornaments, clothing, capes, and even decorative designs could be worn. Each class and occupation had its own designated garments and insignia. For the rulers were reserved the right

> to wear the fine mantles of cotton embroidered with designs and threads of different colors and featherwork. . . .

> Only the king and the sovereigns of the provinces and other great lords are to wear gold arm-bands, anklets, and golden rattles on their feet at the dances.[21]

Thus Moctezuma, visually as well as legally, reinforced the distinctions between classes. The ruler and nobles in Aztec society were the recipients of the empire's wealth. They owned land and controlled the laborers who worked it. They managed important resources such as gold mines, obsidian quarries, and trade routes; and shared with the ruler in the rich tribute from the conquered states. Nobles also received tribute from the lower classes of the city and countryside. This local tribute

45. *Nezahualpilli (from the* Codex Ixtlilxochitl).

46. *Tocuepotzin (from the* Codex Ixtlilxochitl).

was paid in the form of personal services, food, and the labor necessary to build and maintain the temples, palaces, and public works of Tenochtitlan.

Members of the nobility had special privileges. They lived in splendid houses with many servants and possessed expensive luxuries such as fine food, elegant clothes, works of art, and magnificent jewelry. In their leisure time they enjoyed feasts, games and gambling, art, music, drama, and poetry. Their sons were trained in elite temple schools (calmecac), where they learned the military arts, religion, law, history, the calendar, oral literature, and writing.

Girls of noble birth might also attend temple schools, but their lives were primarily concerned with the home, where they learned to direct servants in household tasks and to weave beautiful cotton textiles. Their marriages were carefully arranged to increase the wealth and power of their families. The giving and taking of women in marriage was a vital part of state alliances. Sisters and daughters of the nobility were wed to foreign rulers to solidify relationships and to add the Aztec bloodline to neighboring royal families.

As educated adults, noblemen served the ruler and empire as ambassadors, tax collectors, provincial governors, teachers, scribes, judges, priests, and generals. Ideally, if not always in practice, nobles were expected to lead exemplary lives and were more sternly punished for crimes than were members of the lower classes.

Although described by the Spanish as a man of simple habits, Moctezuma lived in lavish style in his magnificent palace and was waited on by a multitude of servants. He dressed in the finest cotton garments and wore elaborate jewelry. On his head, he wore a mosaic diadem inlaid with precious turquoise; on his feet, he wore sandals of gold. Bernal Díaz tells how his meals were prepared and served.

> For each meal his servants prepared him more than thirty dishes . . . which they put over small earthenware braziers to prevent them from getting cold. They cooked more than three hundred plates of food . . . fowls, turkeys . . . wild ducks, venison . . .
>
> . . . .
>
> [his] food was served on Cholula ware, some red and some black . . . Sometimes they brought him in cups of pure gold a drink made from the cocoa-plant . . . all frothed up, of which he would drink a little.[22]

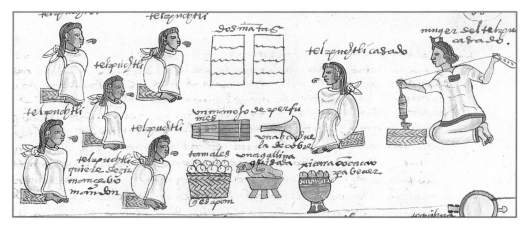

When banquets were given by the nobility, no expense was spared. Torches shown brightly in the night; rich dishes of turkey, duck, dog, and fish were served with tamales of many kinds, fruits, and gourds of frothing whipped chocolate to drink. Pipes of tobacco were passed around after the meal.

47. Banquet scene (from the Codex Mendoza).

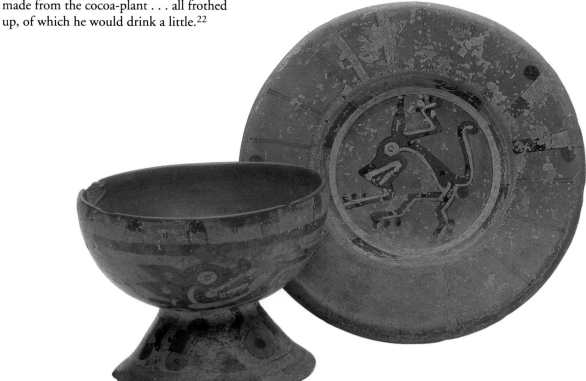

48. Plate and Cup
ceramic
plate: 1 ³/₁₀. diameter 8 ⁴/₅ inches
(03.3, diameter 22.5 cm)
cup: 4 ²/₅. diameter 6 ²/₅ inches
(11.2, diameter 15.8 cm)

Aztec nobles used fine polychrome Cholula ware to serve food and beverages.

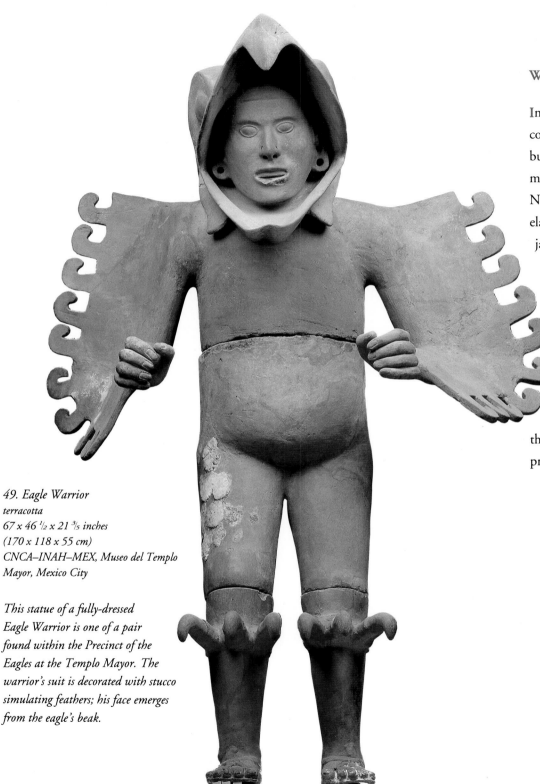

49. Eagle Warrior
terracotta
67 x 46 1/2 x 21 3/5 inches
(170 x 118 x 55 cm)
CNCA–INAH–MEX, Museo del Templo
Mayor, Mexico City

This statue of a fully-dressed
Eagle Warrior is one of a pair
found within the Precinct of the
Eagles at the Templo Mayor. The
warrior's suit is decorated with stucco
simulating feathers; his face emerges
from the eagle's beak.

WARFARE

In Aztec society, all able men—nobles and commoners alike—were trained to be warriors, but only members of the nobility made up the military orders of Eagle and Jaguar Warriors. Noblemen belonging to these elite units wore elaborate costumes and plumage depicting eagles or jaguars. Special quarters were established for them in the sacred precinct near the Templo Mayor. There they gathered for feasts and rituals connected with warfare. These esteemed warriors participated in the wars of conquest and in the eternal cycle of battle, capture, and human sacrifice that was at the heart of the Aztec world. These courageous warriors knew and accepted that fate might dictate that they too, as warriors of the sun, could be taken prisoner and be offered as sacrifice to foreign gods.

From where the eagles are resting,
from where the tigers are exalted,
the Sun is invoked.
. . . .
This is Your Command
oh Giver of Life!
. . . .
With our arrows,
with our shields,
The City exists.
Mexico-Tenochtitlan remains.[23]

50. Warfare
pastel on paper
36 x 44 inches (91 x 112 cm)

Dressed in elaborate costumes, warriors
fought in fierce hand-to-hand combat.

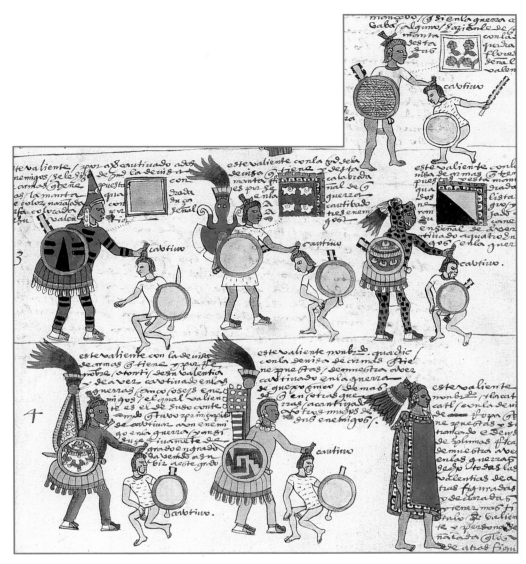

Aztec warfare—economic, political, and religious in nature—had two major goals. The first goal was to expand the borders of the Aztec empire and to bring wealth into the capital. The second was to provide sacrificial victims for the gods, and through the victims' ritual deaths, demonstrate the power of the conquerors. Thus in battle, the intent of a warrior was not to kill his enemy but to take him alive to Tenochtitlan to be offered in sacrifice on top of one of the towering pyramids. Adulation and the award of special favors, wealth, and insignia from the hands of the emperor were the rewards for taking prisoners.

At times, when large numbers of human sacrifices were to be offered in Tenochtitlan, rulers of the conquered city-state that provided the sacrificial victims through war or tribute were invited to view the ceremonies. As a new temple was dedicated or a new ruler crowned, the tributary rulers were given a place of honor to observe the elaborate sacrificial rituals that symbolized the power of the Aztec state and its gods.

51. The Codex Mendoza *illustrates the progression of privileged costumes that awaited the warrior who took one, two, three, four, or more prisoners in battle. The warrior's elaborately decorated long cloak and jewelry reminded all who saw him of his accomplishments in war and his contribution to Aztec society.*

The nobility of the Aztec world took great delight in games, particularly the ancient Mesoamerican ball-game called *tlachtli*. The origins of the game lie deep in the past—as early as the Olmecs of 1000 B.C. The sport was played on an I-shaped, whitewashed stucco court made up of two long, parallel walls with stone rings attached high up at the center points. Players attempted to hit a solid rubber ball through one of the stone rings, using only the hips, buttocks, and knees—not with the hands. Players were specially trained for the game and wore heavy gloves, wide belts, and padded hip guards to protect themselves from injury. The Spanish friar Diego Durán describes the action:

> On seeing the ball come at them, at the moment that it was about to touch the floor, they [the players] were so quick in turning their knees or buttocks to the ball that they returned it with an extraordinary swiftness. With this bouncing back and forth they suffered terrible injuries on their knees or thighs.[24]

Playing tlachtli was generally reserved for the nobility or for professionally trained teams sponsored by the nobility. The outcome of the game was thought to be determined by the gods; it was a game of divine chance and often was used to make decisions about future events. Although basically a religious ritual, the game also was an entertaining spectator sport. Nobles bet heavily and wagered their clothing, jewelry, land, mistresses, and even their freedom in

the fervor of the game. The popularity and importance of the sport is documented by the demand in the tribute lists for 16,000 rubber balls to be delivered each year to Tenochtitlan by communities in the rubber-growing lands to the east. As in the sports world today, the winners were honored as heroes. According to Durán,

> The man who sent the ball through the stone ring was surrounded by all. They honored him, sang songs of praise to him, and joined him in dancing. He was given a very special reward of feathers or mantles and breechcloths, something highly prized. But what he most prized was the honor involved: that was his great wealth. For he was honored as a man who had vanquished many and had won a battle.[25]

52. *The ancient ball game of tlachtli, as shown in this image from the* Codex Magliabecchiano, *was played on an I-shaped court with stone rings mounted on the walls.*

53. Patolli players prayed to the
patron god of games Macuilxochitl.
In this drawing from the Codex
Magliabecchiano, patolli players
invoke good luck from the god.

Another game of chance, *patolli*, was enjoyed by
all—rich and poor alike. Played with a set of smooth
pebbles on a mat marked with a large **X** that was
divided into 52 boxes, the game was similar to the
modern game of Parcheesi. Beans painted with white
dots to indicate numbers were used as dice. Red and
blue pebbles were moved around the board according
to the throw of the beans. Some people became
addicted to the game. Durán tells us:

> The gamblers dedicated to this game always
> went about with the mats under their
> armpits and with the dice tied up in small
> cloths . . . it was believed that [the dice]
> were mighty . . . they spoke to them and
> begged them to be favorable, to come to
> their aid in that game.[26]

For entertainment Moctezuma and his nobles
enjoyed hunting in their gardens and parks. Birds
often were hunted with blowpipes. Sahagún
mentions that bows and arrows or spears were
used for target shooting. Hunts for larger game,
such as deer, wild dogs, and rabbits, were organized
in the forest. Beaters drove the game into a central
area where it was killed. These special hunts often
were held during *Quecholli*, a special period of the
year dedicated to *Mixcoatl*, god of the hunt. At
these gatherings, the ruler invited successful hunters
to a feast.

Out of the continual round of battle and death, demanding gods, and the rigid structure of society grew a fatalistic view of life and the universe. This world view is reflected in a rich tradition of magnificent Nahuatl poetry. To the great Aztec poets and philosophers, the beyond was unknown. Reality and beauty were only for the moment.

> Truly do we live on earth?
> Not forever on earth; only a little while here.
> Although it be jade, it will be broken,
> Although it be gold, it is crushed,
> Although it be quetzal feather, it is torn asunder.
> Not forever on earth; only a little while here.[27]

In the Aztec world, ideas and thoughts were not recorded by the written word, but in a series of standardized pictures that served as memory devices for a splendid oral tradition. Aztec books, called codices, were made from deerskin or bark paper. They were screen folded or rolled rather than bound, and painted in bright colors. In these ancient manuscripts, priests and scribes recorded poetry, history, rituals, tribute lists, and rhetoric that was recited or read by those trained in the temple schools to write and interpret them. Greatly revered in Aztec society, these priests and scribes were considered descendants of the Toltecs.

> Those who
> carried with them
> the black and red ink,
> the manuscripts and the pictures,
> wisdom. . . .
> They brought everything with them:
> the song books and the music of the flutes.[28]

Aztec Religion

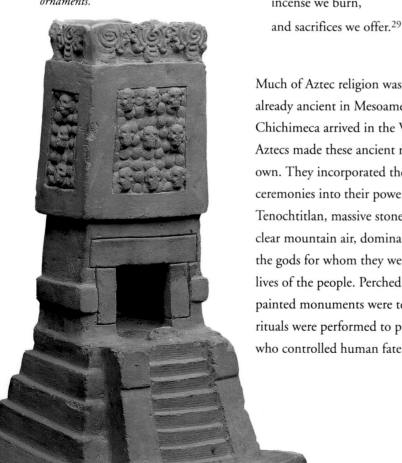

54. Temple Model
ceramic
12 ⁴/₅ x 6 ¹/₂ inches (32.5 x 16.5 cm)
*CNCA–INAH–MEX, Museo Nacional de
Antropología, Mexico City*

*This model shows in remarkable detail
the appearance of temples throughout
Tenochtitlan. Stairs lead to the platform
on which a sacrificial stone was placed in
front of the entrance. The upper walls
are decorated with skulls; the roof is
crowned with shell-shaped architectural
ornaments.*

From [our ancestors] have we inherited

our pattern of life

. . . .

They taught us

all their rules of worship,

all their ways of honoring the gods.

Thus before them, do we prostrate
   ourselves;

in their names we bleed ourselves;
   our oaths we keep,

incense we burn,

and sacrifices we offer.[29]

Much of Aztec religion was based on traditions already ancient in Mesoamerica when the first Chichimeca arrived in the Valley of Mexico. The Aztecs made these ancient rites and ceremonies their own. They incorporated the earlier gods and ceremonies into their powerful pantheon. In Tenochtitlan, massive stone pyramids rose in the clear mountain air, dominating the landscape just as the gods for whom they were built dominated the lives of the people. Perched on top of these brightly painted monuments were temples where elaborate rituals were performed to placate the powerful deities who controlled human fate and destiny.

New gods were constantly being added to the Aztec pantheon from conquered city-states. These foreign deities were brought to dwell in Tenochtitlan to add their power to the Aztec empire. To ensure that the gods were favorably inclined toward the needs of humans, the Aztecs performed ceremonies in the gods' honor that included offerings of incense, flowers, birds, and animals as well as the sacrifice of humans, whose hearts and blood were considered the supreme gift.

Religion permeated the daily experience of all Aztecs—nobles and commoners alike. Throughout the religious calendar people were called upon to participate in colorful performances that pleased and empowered the demanding gods. Performed in the open, on the steps of the pyramids, and in the great plazas, these ceremonies included musicians who played flutes, drums, bells, and conch shell trumpets, and dancers who wound their way around pyramids and through the city's streets. Poetry was chanted and sung to the gods; ritual dramas, often ending in human sacrifices, were enacted with performers and god impersonators dressed in elaborate costumes. These ceremonies, with their ritual human sacrifices and offerings, were the symbolic link through which the Aztecs sought to propitiate their gods.

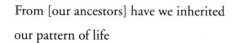

Following ancient customs, priests led the Aztec people in the offering of blood sacrifice to the gods—both from their own bodies and from sacrificial victims. Priests taught the dances, music, and drama that accompanied the ceremonies and through the teaching and transmission of the rich oral traditions, ensured that the ancient songs and rituals would endure.

Thousands of priests served Aztec religion at temples such as the Templo Mayor. The priesthood was organized into different levels. Novice priests lived at the temple school in austere conditions. They rose before dawn to perform menial labor and practice autosacrifice (the drawing of their own blood by piercing their skin with maguey cactus spines). Rising in rank about every five years, priests eventually became "fire givers" and were allowed to perform human sacrifice. Experienced priests taught at the temple schools and lived together within the temple precincts.

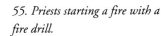

All priests followed a rigidly structured daily routine of duties that included sweeping the temples, making offerings, burning incense, keeping the temple fires burning, fasting, and performing penance—including autosacrifice. They also blew conch shell trumpets at ritual times throughout the day and night.

55. Priests starting a fire with a fire drill.

56. Priest carrying an incense brazier (from the Codex Mendoza*).*

Like members of the Aztec nobility, priests were recognized by their physical appearance. Some painted their bodies black with soot from head to toe. They wore their hair long—at times down to their knees—tied back with a white ribbon. They smeared their foreheads with their own blood and wore special fringed, sleeveless tunics that reached the knees. They carried an incense burner, a bag of incense, and a gourd for tobacco.

57. Incense Braziers
ceramic with polychrome
top: 3 ²/₅ x 26, diameter 10 ²/₅ inches
(8.6 x 66, diameter 26.5 cm)
bottom: 3 x 24 ¹/₂, diameter 9 inches
(7.7 x 61.5, diameter 22.8 cm)
CNCA–INAH–MEX, Museo Nacional de Antropología, Mexico City

These Cholula ware incense braziers with long handles were carried by priests in processions. The crosses and holes cut in the bottoms of the braziers symbolize Xiuhtecuhtli, the old god of fire.

58. Aztec musicians (from the Florentine Codex).

59. Incense Brazier with Head of Fertility God
ceramic
21 x 26 inches (53.7 x 66 cm)
CNCA–INAH–MEX, Museo Nacional de Antropología, Mexico City

60. Drum
wood
9 ²/₅ (width) x 26 ²/₅ (length) inches (24 x 67 cm)
CNCA–INAH–MEX, Museo Nacional de Antropología, Mexico City

This wooden drum with the face of a jaguar and stylized ducks on the sides was carved from a solid piece of hardwood. It was played with rubber-tipped wooden sticks. The two "tongues" of wood on the top produced different tones when struck.

[The priests] went about . . . blackened, and wasted and haggard of face. They wore their hair hanging down very long . . . so that it covered them. . . . At night they walked like a procession of phantoms to the hills where they had their temples and idols and houses of worship.[30]

The burning of incense to the gods—in temples, shrines, and homes—was common in Aztec religion. The most frequently used incense was copal, which was made from the resin of conifer trees. Incense was offered in all ritual ceremonies and four times during the day and five times at night:

The first time . . . when it was dark. The second time was when it was time to go to sleep. The third time was when the shell trumpets were sounded. The fourth time was at midnight. And the fifth time was near dawn.[31]

Long-handled, ceramic incense burners were used in ritual incense ceremonies performed by priests. Priests scooped burning coals into the brazier, sprinkled the coals with incense, and then raised the billowing incense overhead to the four directions. The incense and burning coals were then thrown into a brazier where they continued to burn.

The great temples of Tenochtitlan were never silent; every religious ceremony incorporated music and drama. Singers and dancers were accompanied by flutes,

conch shell trumpets, ceramic and wooden drums, rattles, rasps, copper bells, and whistles. Dancers and actors sometimes dressed in colorful costumes portraying the gods or creatures such as butterflies, hummingbirds, and jaguars.

All boys and girls between the ages of 12 and 15 attended a house of song where they learned to sing, dance, and play musical instruments. Through songs, Aztec youth learned traditional views of the gods and legends of creation, life, and death. Some students became professional singers and dancers—vocations highly esteemed by the Aztecs.

At the heart of Aztec religion was the belief that in the past, the world was created and destroyed by the gods on four separate occasions. At the end of each era, the sun and all the creatures on earth were demolished by catastrophic events such as floods or winds. After each destruction the earth had to be created once again. The Aztecs believed that their own world, the Fifth Sun, was created at the ancient site of Teotihuacan by an old, diseased god who had the courage to fling himself into the fire to be resurrected as the sun.

> this is our Sun,
> in which we now live,
> and this is its sign,
> where the Sun fell in fire
> on the divine hearth,
> there in Teotihuacan.[32]

This new sun at first was unable to move across the heavens. The other gods finally sacrificed themselves and provided their own blood as sustenance for the sun's movement. The human sacrifices, which were the focal point of so many Aztec religious rituals, symbolized the continual effort of the Aztec people to repay this blood debt to the gods. As people of the sun, the Aztecs were responsible for continually supplying the blood of human sacrifices. This divine offering provided the energy for the sun to move across the sky and prevented the world of the Fifth Sun from coming to an end.

61. New Fire Ceremony
pastel on paper
56 x 36 inches (142.2 x 91.4 cm)

62. Starting the new fire on the chest of a sacrificial victim (from the Florentine Codex*).*

It was the doctrine of the elders

that there is life because of the gods;

with their sacrifice, they gave us life.

. . . .

When there was still darkness.[33]

To postpone the foretold destruction of the Fifth Sun by earthquakes, the Aztecs performed the New Fire Ceremony once every 52 years at the completion of a calendar cycle (a period of time conceptually equivalent to our century).

On the day of the ceremony, all fires in the Valley of Mexico were extinguished. Household goods, cooking pots, and hearthstones were thrown away. All homes were swept clean, inside and out. At dusk, everyone climbed to their rooftops to watch and wait in the dark, trembling with fear at their uncertain future. Small children were kept awake; parents feared they would turn into mice if they fell asleep.

At sunset, a solemn procession of priests dressed as gods traveled to the Hill of the Star south of Tenochtitlan. Arriving at the summit, they carefully watched for the constellation Pleiades to climb to its zenith in the night sky. When the observers were assured that the heavens would continue to rotate, an honored priest started a new fire on the chest of a specially selected captive.

The captive's heart was then torn from his chest and thrown into the fire. A cry of relief rose throughout the Valley when people saw the flickering flames. Swift runners carried torches lighted from the ceremonial fire to the Templo Mayor in the center of Tenochtitlan, where a fire was started before a statue of Huitzilopochtli. New fires were then taken to temples and homes throughout the city.

The last Aztec New Fire Ceremony occurred in 1507, during the reign of Moctezuma II.

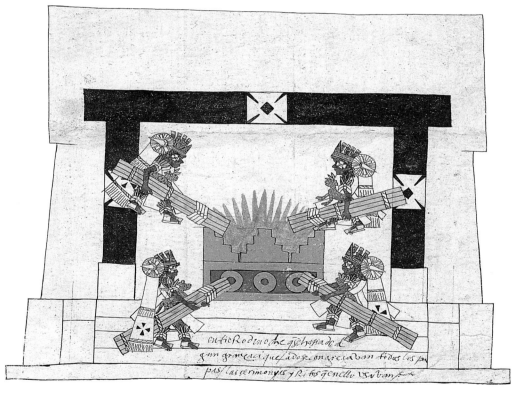

63. Priests light bundles of 52 sticks to carry the new fire to Tenochtitlan (from the Codex Borbonicus*).*

More generally, Aztec religion focused on three themes of prime importance. Each theme incorporated a group of anthropomorphic deities (gods imbued with human traits) who required constant nourishment. The themes were primordial creation, fertility and rain, and warfare.

Living at the summit of the world was the primordial force, a deity who combined both male and female characteristics in one being. All other gods and humans descended from this being.

Closely associated with this creation deity was Tezcatlipoca, "the God of Gods," Lord of the Smoking Mirror, and the patron god of Aztec rulers. He was seen as the virile and ever-young warrior. Tezcatlipoca was the god of everywhere; he ruled in the land of the dead, on earth, and in heaven. His obsidian mirror allowed him to see all things in all places. All creatures were helpless before him.

Tezcatlipoca was honored at a yearly ceremony in which a handsome young male was chosen from a group of captive warriors to impersonate the god. The chosen one was as follows:

like something smoothed, like a tomato . . . as if sculptured in wood . . . his hair was indeed straight . . . [and] long. He . . . had no pimples on his forehead . . . He was not long-headed . . . he was not swollen-cheeked . . . he was not flat-nosed . . . He was not thick-lipped . . . he was not a stutterer . . . his teeth were [like] seashells . . . he was not poor of vision . . . Nor was he large-eared . . . He was not emaciated; he was not fat. . . [He] had no flaw . . . no [bodily] defects . . . no blemish . . . no mark.[34]

64. Mirror and Flute
mirror: obsidian
³⁄₈. diameter 7 ³⁄₁₀ inches
(1.6, diameter 18.5 cm)
flute: clay
22 ²⁄₅ (width) x 9 ³⁄₅ (length) inches
(3.9, 24.5 cm)
CNCA–INAH–MEX, Museo Nacional de Antropología, Mexico City

These two objects are intimately associated with Tezcatlipoca. His omniscience is symbolized by the obsidian mirror that allowed him to see everyone and everything in all places. The flute decorated with a flower is typical of those played, then broken, by the god impersonator as he climbed the steep temple steps to his death.

65. As seen in this image from the Florentine Codex, *broken flutes litter the steps leading to the temple where the impersonator of Tezcatlipoca was sacrificed.*

66. *Lidded Vessel with Figure of Tezcatlipoca*
orange ceramic
vessel: 13, diameter 6 ⁴/₅ inches
(33.2, diameter 17.4 cm)
lid: ¹/₂, diameter 7 ¹/₅ inches
(1.2, diameter 18.2 cm)
CNCA–INAH–MEX, Museo del Templo Mayor, Mexico City

This vessel is decorated with a relief sculpture of Tezcatlipoca armed with a spear thrower and two spears. An undulating serpent with open mouth is carved into the background. When found beneath the front platform on the Huitzilopochtli side of the Templo Mayor, the vessel contained remains of human bones and obsidian beads.

The young impersonator lived in luxury for one year. He learned to play the flute, to hold a smoking tube, to carry flowers, and to speak graciously. Throughout the year, he moved freely about the city, accompanied by a specially selected entourage. All those he met bowed before him and greeted him as the god himself.

During the year, the impersonator was taken before Moctezuma, who adorned the youth with all manner of precious gifts: gold and turquoise ornaments for his ears, a seashell necklace and breastplate, a snail shell lip pendant, gold and turquoise bracelets, a net cape of the finest brown cotton, gold bells for his legs, and obsidian sandals.

Twenty days prior to the ceremony, the impersonator was stripped of his precious ornaments and dressed as a warrior. He was given four wives with whom he lived until the day of his death.

On the day of the ceremony, the youth was escorted to a small temple south of Tenochtitlan.

Alone he ascended the steep pyramid steps, breaking a flute on each step as he climbed toward his death on the sacrificial stone—a god, sacrificed in honor of the god.

Immediately upon the impersonator's death, another physically attractive youth was selected to impersonate the god—the ritual cycle started over again.

Also associated with the creator god was the old god of fire, Xiuhtecuhtli. He was among the oldest of Mesoamerican gods. When the Aztecs adopted this god from the ancient cultures that preceded them, he became the symbol of the ancient yet eternal fire that ensures life to the people.

Fire was important to the Aztecs in all aspects of their lives, both in their homes and temples. Fire provided warmth and heat for cooking. New homes were dedicated by building a fire in the hearth surrounded by three hearthstones. During a wedding ceremony, the bride walked around the hearth fire seven times. Eternal fires were kept burning in temple braziers throughout Tenochtitlan. Fire played a prominent role in many rituals dedicated to the gods, including the fire god, Xiuhtecuhtli himself.

67. Fire surrounded by three hearth stones formed the heart of an Aztec home (from the Florentine Codex).

68. Xiuhtecuhtli
volcanic stone
19 ⅛ x 8 ⅝ inches (48.5 x 22 cm)
CNCA–INAH–MEX, Museo Nacional de Antropología, Mexico City

This statue shows the old fire god with a wrinkled brow and only two teeth—Aztec symbols of old age. His physical strength belies his advanced years. At one time, shell or obsidian was inlaid in the eyes, giving the sculpture a realistic appearance.

69. Xiuhtecuhtli
stone with polychrome
17 x 7 ⁴/₅ inches (43.3 x 20 cm)
CNCA–INAH–MEX, Museo Nacional de
Antropología, Mexico City

*In this statue, Xiuhtecuhtli, also known
as the Turquoise Lord, wears his
traditional headdress of two protruding
disks. The disks symbolize beams of
wood that were rubbed together to
make fire. Like the other statue of
Xiuhtecuhtli, he also has only two teeth.
The turquoise color shows an association
with the rain god, Tlaloc.*

*This magnificent stone sculpture retains
some of the original paint that once
adorned almost all Aztec sculptures.
Most of the colorful finish has been worn
away by the ravages of time.*

The second theme in Aztec religion concerned fertility and rain. More ceremonies and sacrifices were connected with the crucial needs of agriculture than with any other aspect of Aztec life. The deities of the earth, maize, sexuality, and fertility in general were worshiped in this category.

Tlaloc, the god of rain, was the most important of the deities associated with this theme.

> To him was attributed the rain; for he created, brought down, showered down the rain and the hail. He caused the trees, the grasses, the maize to blossom, to sprout, to leaf out, to bloom, to grow.[35]

Tlaloc was a beneficial god. But when angered, he was greatly feared. He could unleash floods and cause lightning, thunder, and hail. He also could stop the rains, causing life-threatening drought. To placate Tlaloc's wrath, the most precious gift of all, the lives of infants and children were offered to him. Children born under a special day sign and those who had a swirling cowlick in their hair were dedicated from infancy to be participants in the rituals. For some sacrifices, children who were bought as slaves sufficed; certain ceremonies, however, required the sacrifice of children of noble birth. Thus for the sake of the essential rains and a continual food supply, sacrifice was demanded of all classes of people.

70. Box Fragment with Image of Tlaloc
stone
11 ²/₅ x 13 ⁴/₅ inches (29 x 35 cm)
CNCA–INAH–MEX, Museo Nacional de Antropología, Mexico City

This bottom fragment of a stone box shows Tlaloc wearing his characteristic goggle mask made up of two snakes coiled around his eyes. His large fangs also are easily seen.

Also associated with fertility was Xipe Totec, "Our
Lord the Flayed One," the god of early spring, and
the patron god of goldworkers. His cult was one of
the most unusual in the Aztec pantheon. It involved
flaying and wearing a human skin, which symbolized
the earth covering itself with new springtime
vegetation and thus exchanging old skin for new.

During the ceremony, prisoners who had dis-
tinguished themselves in battle were taken one by
one to fight for their lives. With an ankle tied to a
stone, each was to defend
himself with a feather-covered
wooden club and four heavy

wooden balls. Each captive in turn fought four brave
Eagle and Jaguar Warriors. If the prisoner somehow
managed to defeat these well-armed warriors, a fifth
was sent to kill him. (Legend tells of a famous
Tlaxcalteca warrior named Tlahuicole who, after
given command of an Aztec army against the
Tarascans, asked to participate in this gladiatorial
combat. Before he was sacrificed, he killed 8 warriors
and wounded 20 others.)

When all the captives were killed, their skins
were removed to be worn by Xipe impersonators.
The captive's skin was stretched tightly across the
wearer's face like a mask; the hands and feet dangled
uselessly at the impersonator's wrists and ankles.
Impersonators wore the skins for 20 days while they
roamed the city's streets, begging for food and gifts.
Finally at a great feast, the skins were removed and
buried in a secret, underground vault.

Human sacrifice was a fundamental part of Aztec religion. The Aztecs believed that as the people of the sun, they were responsible for sustaining the sun and thus maintaining life for all humankind. Only the most precious liquid—human blood—could sustain the sun each day on its journey across the sky. The welfare of the earth's people and the Aztec empire were dependent upon the sacred rite of human sacrifice.

Human sacrifice was a deeply religious act. All sacrifices took place in a sacred context. Hatred and anger were not components of such ceremonies. The sacrificial victim was seen not only as an offering to the gods but as a messenger as well. When people died in sacrifice, they died as gods—an honor that was reported to have been accepted willingly and proudly in the colorful drama of the rituals. The sacrifice of a courageous warrior was more nourishing to the gods than the sacrifice of a slave.

72. When a human was sacrificed to the gods, the body was laid over a sacrificial stone. As shown in the Florentine Codex, *four priests then held the captive's arms and legs while a fifth priest, using a sharp knife, opened the chest and removed the heart.*

73. Vessels with Skull Decorations
ceramic
11 2/5 x 4 9/10 inches (29 x 12.5 cm)
CNCA–INAH–MEX, Museo Nacional de Antropología, Mexico City

These beautiful Cholula ware vessels decorated with three-dimensional skulls probably were used in religious rituals concerned with death and human sacrifice.

Gods associated with the theme of warfare regularly demanded offerings of human sacrifices. Much of this divine nourishment was supplied in the form of captives taken in battle. Huitzilopochtli, the supreme god of warriors, was the most important deity to the Aztecs. As their ancient patron god, he was associated with warfare and the sun. He continually encouraged the Aztecs in their wars of aggression and was fed the blood of their sacrifices.

74. Sacrificial Knife (reproduction)
wood blade and handle with turquoise and shell mosaic
3 ⁹/₁₀ x 8 ³/₁₀ inches (10 x 21 cm)
CNCA–INAH–MEX, Museo Nacional de Antropología, Mexico City

This sacrificial knife with a turquoise and shell mosaic handle in the shape of a warrior is a reproduction of those used to perform human sacrifice. The knife was reproduced by the National Museum of Anthropology in Mexico City during the late 1940s.

Huitzilopochtli, the young warrior,
who acts above! He follows his path!
"Not in vain did I dress myself in yellow
    plumes,
for I am he who has caused the sun
    to rise."[36]

In connection with the sacrifice of warriors taken in battle and offered to Huitzilopochtli, evidence exists that some ceremonies involved the ritual consumption of human flesh. After a prisoner's heart had been removed and dedicated to the sun, the body was claimed by the warrior who had captured him. The legs and arms were cooked and eaten by the warrior's relatives in a ritual feast to honor the victim's courage and sacrifice. The captor himself, however, never partook of the meal. A mystic kinship existed between captive and captor—one that made them ritually as close as father and son.

75. In this drawing from the Codex Borbonicus, *Mictlantecuhtli is shown with his body covered with human bones. He wears a mask made from a human skull and a human bone as an earplug. His curled black hair is decorated with paper rosettes.*

76. *Mictlantecuhtli*
travertine marble
6 ³/₅ x 3 ⁷/₁₀ inches (16.8 x 9.5 cm)
CNCA–INAH–MEX, Museo Nacional de Antropología, Mexico City

This beautifully carved vase shows Mictlantecuhtli, the lord of the underworld and patron god of the dead. He wears a headdress with an enormous feather, a necklace of human hearts, and long cloth earrings that symbolize death and the underworld. His bulging eyes stare out through a skull mask.

Cihuateteo were the spirits of women who died in childbirth. Because they died producing a new life for the empire, they were considered equal to warriors killed in battle or on the sacrificial stone. Like warriors, they had an important role in the daily movement of the sun across the sky. Warriors carried the sun from the dawn in the east to its zenith. Cihuateteo carried the sun from its zenith to its setting in the west.

The goddesses were terrifying and greatly feared. On five special days of the year, they haunted crossroads, hoping to kidnap or maim a child. Fearful mothers kept their children inside at night and set up shrines to appease these frightening spirits. This statue was probably placed in a shrine.

77. Cihuateotl
volcanic stone
28 x 18 ⁷/₈ x 17 ³/₈ inches
(71 x 48 x 44 cm)
CNCA–INAH–MEX, Museo Nacional de
Antropología, Mexico City

This statue of cihuateotl shows the goddess with long, matted hair (an Aztec symbol of death); an open mouth with prominent teeth; large, round eyes staring out of her skull; and clenched claws that add to her fearsome appearance. She wears an unadorned skirt and circular earplugs.

78. *Quetzalcoatl, the Feathered Serpent*
stone
9 ⁷/₈, diameter 15 ³/₄ inches
(25, diameter 40 cm)
CNCA–INAH–MEX, Museo Nacional
de Antropología, Mexico City

Feathers that appear to be blown by a
gentle breeze are delicately carved on this
sculpture of Quetzalcoatl, which also
shows the serpent's fangs and large
forked tongue.

None of the themes of Aztec religion completely encompasses Quetzalcoatl, one of the best known of the ancient Mesoamerican gods. Adopted by the Aztecs from the Toltecs, Quetzalcoatl was symbolized by a plumed serpent whose characteristics of both a snake and a bird made him equally at home in the realms of the earth and sky. The Aztecs considered Quetzalcoatl a great culture hero, who was responsible for creating the people of the Fifth Sun. To do this, Quetzalcoatl journeyed to the underworld and brought back the bones of the dead, which he sprinkled with his own blood to create the human race. He also gave humans the precious gift of corn, which was being hoarded by red ants in the center of Tonacatepetl, the Hill of Sustenance.

By changing himself into a black ant, Quetzalcoatl entered the mountain and brought back a few kernels of maize for the gods to sample.

Quetzalcoatl had many personalities. As Ehecatl, god of the wind, he was associated with rain and fertility. As the morning star, Venus, he was associated with warfare. Quetzalcoatl also was the god of learning, culture, and civilization itself. He introduced the calendar and taught the arts of featherworking, metallurgy, and writing. Human sacrifices were rarely offered to Quetzalcoatl. Instead, his followers gave him gifts of incense, flowers, and birds.

79. Xolotl
stone
19 ⁷/₁₀ x 23 ³/₅ inches (50 x 60 cm)
CNCA–INAH–MEX, Museo Nacional de
Antropología, Mexico City

This sculpture of Xolotl's head shows parallel lines creasing the forehead and an open mouth with large teeth and a broad tongue. Xolotl wears ear ornaments associated with the feathered serpent Quetzalcoatl.

In Aztec culture, art and religion were not easily separated. Art was used as a language to communicate the standardized concepts of religion. In Tenochtitlan splendid stone sculptures of the gods were created in a commanding, formal style and placed in the temples and public plazas of the city. The accoutrements and symbols of each god were carefully portrayed and could be recognized by worshipers—the feathers and scales of the plumed serpent Quetzalcoatl, the human skin worn by Xipe Totec, the obsidian mirror and flute of Tezcatlipoca, and the golden bells that adorned the cheeks of the moon goddess Coyolxauhqui.

Although most art was spiritually oriented, some sculptures had no obvious religious symbolism. Aztec artists took great care to portray the special traits of the creatures who shared their natural world. On serpents they carefully carved rattles, scales, and fangs; on jaguars they sculpted spotted pelts and a sensuously curved body line; and on eagles they carved feathers and a cruel beak.

> What is carved should be like the original, and have life, for whatever may be the subject which is to be made, the form of it should resemble the original . . .Take care to penetrate what the animal you wish to imitate is like, and how its character and appearance can best be shown.[37]

Aztec sculptors used only simple stone and wood tools, bird bones, fiber cords, water, and sand to carve hard volcanic stone. These artistic masterpieces represent the efforts of some of the finest artists of Precolumbian America.

Xolotl was the god of twins and monsters, a patron god of the ballgame, and the dog who guided souls of the dead on their journey to the underworld. Xolotl, the evening star, was the twin of Quetzalcoatl, the morning star.

The Templo Mayor: Heart of the Aztec Empire

This Temple was divided at the top so that it appeared to be two, and it had two shrines or altars at the summit. . . . In one of these shrines. . . was the statue of Huitzilopochtli. . . . In the other, there was an image of the god Tlaloc. Before each one of these [images] there was a round stone like a chopping block, called *techcatl*, upon which they killed those who were sacrificed in honor of that god. And from these [sacrificial] stones to the base of the Temple flowed a stream of blood from those [victims] who were slain on them.[38]

In the sacred walled precinct in the middle of Tenochtitlan stood the Templo Mayor. This structure was the actual and symbolic center of the capital city—the heart of the Aztec world. The Templo Mayor, whose twin form dominated the skyline of the metropolis, was dedicated to the worship of the two gods who represented the power sources of the Aztec empire—Huitzilopochtli and Tlaloc—gods of war and rain, of tribute and sustenance. The two halves of the magnificent pyramid represent two sacred mountains. As one faces the temple, on the right is the Hill of Coatepec, where Huitzilopochtli defeated the enemies of the sun. On the left is Tonacatepetl, the Hill of Sustenance, whose patron deity was Tlaloc.

80. *The Great Temple of Texcoco, as shown here in the* Codex Ixtlilxochitl, *was almost identical to the Templo Mayor located in Tenochtitlan.*

81. If standing today, the Templo Mayor would be east of the Metropolitan Cathedral and adjacent to the main plaza, or Zócalo, in modern Mexico City.

The temple pyramid inhabited by the two great deities—Tlaloc and Huitzilopochtli—was a distinctly Aztec architectural design. The stepped pyramid form was an ancient tradition, but the division of that form into a pyramid with two flights of stairs leading to double temples on top was unique to Aztec culture. Until 1978 when the Templo Mayor was discovered, Aztec architecture of this type was known only from excavations outside Tenochtitlan at other Aztec sites such as Santa Cecilia and Tenayuca.

From Spanish chronicles and occasional archaeological finds, Aztec scholars have long known that the sacred precinct and the Templo Mayor were located near the central plaza—the *Zócalo*—in present-day Mexico City. Buildings constructed in the colonial period (1521–1821) and in modern times cover the structures of ancient Tenochtitlan. For centuries, the Templo Mayor had been buried beneath more recent construction.

On February 21, 1978, electrical workers digging in the central plaza of the city discovered what they described as "the arm of a goddess," and notified the National Institute of Anthropology and History of Mexico. The arm turned out to be part of an immense round stone carved with an image of the dismembered body of Coyolxauhqui, moon goddess and sister of Huitzilopochtli. The serendipitous discovery of this spectacular stone sculpture revealed the precise location of the Templo Mayor and initiated one of the most impressive archaeological excavations ever to take place in Mexico.

82. Coyolxauhqui, Goddess of the Moon
volcanic stone
88 ³/₅ x 79 ¹/₂ x 14 ³/₅ inches
(225 x 202 x 37 cm)
CNCA–INAH–MEX, Museo del Templo
Mayor, Mexico City

This magnificent relief sculpture shows the dismembered body of Coyolxauhqui. Her head is adorned with feathers, earrings, and bells on her cheeks. A double-headed snake threaded through a human skull is tied around her waist. She wears bracelets and anklets on her severed limbs; bones protrude from their ends. Monstrous masks with large fangs are carved at her knees, elbows, and on the heels of her sandals.

The sculpture was originally located at the base of the Huitzilopochtli side of the Templo Mayor, with the head facing toward the stairway. Bodies of sacrificial victims were rolled down the temple stairs to land on the sculpture.

The iconography of the Templo Mayor and the magnificent carved stone found at its base refers to an ancient Aztec legend about the birth of Huitzilopochtli on the Hill of Coatepec.

The legend, based on the records of Sahagún, tells how Huitzilopochtli defeated his 400 brothers—the stars—and his sister Coyolxauhqui—the moon.

On Coatepec, in the direction of Tula,
a woman had been living,
a woman dwelt there
by the name of Coatlicue.

She was the mother of the four hundred Southerners,
and of a sister of one of them
named Coyolxauhqui.

And this Coatlicue was doing penance there,
. . . .
on Coatepec, the Mountain of the Serpent.

And once
as Coatlicue was sweeping
some plumage fell on her,
like a ball of fine feathers.

Coatlicue picked it up at once,
she put it in her bosom.
. . . .
From that moment Coatlicue was pregnant.

When the four hundred Southerners saw
that their mother was pregnant,
they became very angry; they said:

"Who has done this to you?
Who has made you pregnant?
He has insulted us, he has dishonored us."

And their sister Coyolxauhqui
said to them:
"Brothers, she has dishonored us,
we must kill our mother,
. . . .
When Coatlicue discovered this,
she was very frightened,
she was very saddened.

But her son, Huitzilopochtli, who was in her bosom,
comforted her, said to her:

"Don't be afraid.
I know what I must do."
Coatlicue, having heard
the words of her son,
took great comfort,
her heart was calmed,
she felt tranquil.

And meanwhile, the four hundred Southerners
gathered to take council,
and unanimously they agreed
to kill their mother
because she had disgraced them.
. . . .
Coyolxauhqui greatly incited them,
inflamed her brothers' anger,
so they would kill their mother.

. . . .

But one named Cuahuitlicac
was false in his words.

What the four hundred Southerners said
he went to tell it at once,
he went to reveal it to Huitzilopochtli.

And Huitzilopochtli answered:
"Be careful, be alert,
my uncle, I know well what I must do."

And when finally they had agreed,
when the four hundred Southerners were resolved
to kill, to destroy their mother,
. . . .

83. Detail of Coyolxauhqui stone

Then they began to move out,
they went in order, in a row,
in an orderly squadron,
Coyolxauhqui guided them.

But Cuahuitlicac at once went up to mountain
to speak from there to Huitzilopochtli,
he said to him:

"They're coming now."

Huitzilopochtli answered him:
"Look carefully at where they are."

Then Cuahuitlicac said:
"Now they're passing through Tzompantitlan."
. . . .
"Now they are passing through Coaxalpan."
. . . .
"Now they are on the mountain top, they are
    drawing near,
Coyolxauhqui is guiding them."

At that moment Huitzilopochtli was born,
he dressed himself in his finery,
his shield of eagle feathers,
his darts, his blue dart thrower,
the notable turquoise dart thrower.

He painted his face
with diagonal stripes,
with the color called "child's paint."

On his head he placed fine feathers,
he put on his earplugs.

And on one of his feet, the left one was very thin,
he wore a sandal covered with feathers,
and his two legs and his two arms
he had them painted blue.

And the one named Tochancalqui
took out the serpent made of candlewood,
whose name was Xiuhcoatl,
who obeyed Huitzilopochtli.

Then with it he wounded Coyolxauhqui,
he cut off her head,
. . . .
The body of Coyolxauhqui
rolled down the slope,
it fell apart in pieces,
her hands, her legs, her torso
fell in different places.

Then Huitzilopochtli raised up,
he pursued the four hundred Southerners,
he kept on pursuing them, he scattered them
from the top of Coatepetl,
the mountain of the serpent.

. . . .

Huitzilopochtli pursued them, he chased them,
he destroyed them, he annihilated them,
    he obliterated them.
. . . .
And when Huitzilopochtli had killed them,
when he had expressed his anger,
he took from them their finery, their adornments,
their destiny, put them on, appropriated them,
incorporated them into his destiny,
made of them his own insignia.

. . . .

And his cult was taken from there,
from Coatepec, the Mountain of the Serpent,
as it was practiced from times
most ancient.[39]

84. Detail of Coyolxauhqui stone.

85. *María Luisa Franco and Eduardo Matos Moctezuma stabilize the Coyolxauhqui stone.*

The Aztec legend of the birth of Huitzilopochtli clearly relates to the Templo Mayor. The pyramid itself represents the Hill of Coatepec; the carved stone found at its base symbolizes Coyolxauhqui's dismembered body. The defeat of the stars and moon, symbols of darkness and the night sky, by Huitzilopochtli, warrior of the sun, was the epic battle that assured the sun's place in the daytime sky. This legendary battle between the sun and the moon was reenacted in special ceremonies atop the Templo Mayor: a victim was sacrificed, his blood was offered as sustenance to the sun, and his body was thrown down the steep "hill" of the pyramid onto the Coyolxauhqui stone.

And this Huitzilopochtli, as they say,
was a prodigy
. . . .
The Aztecs venerated him,
they made sacrifices to him,
honored and served him.
And Huitzilopochtli rewarded
those who did this.[40]

Archaeologist Eduardo Matos Moctezuma was named director of the Templo Mayor Project. Its goal was the excavation of the magnificent pyramid complex and the interpretation of its objects. An interdisciplinary team of archaeologists, anthropologists, art historians, scholars of religion, ethnohistorians, zoologists, and ethnobotanists worked from 1978 to 1982, carefully uncovering and recording the remains of the Templo Mayor and its thousands of artifacts.

THE BAT GOD

In October 1990, near Chalco, in the southeastern part of Mexico City, a man digging in his backyard discovered terracotta fragments that he realized were part of an animal's face. He continued digging until he found the legs, torso, and head of an ancient sculpture. He reported his significant discovery to the National Institute of Anthropology and History (INAH) in Mexico City.

Archaeologist Francisco Hinojosa carefully examined the surrounding area to determine if the pieces were related to any architectural features and then carefully excavated the sculpture. The excavation revealed the figure of a Bat God lying on its back in a hole beneath fragments of a sculpture of the god Xipe Totec.

When excavation of the two figures was complete, the fragments were sent to the Restoration and Conservation Department of INAH, in Churubusco, Mexico City, where a team of conservators began the painstaking task of reassembling the sculptures.

The nearly 200 pieces of the Bat God were carefully cleaned of the minerals and mud that had accumulated while the figure was buried, and then were strengthened by immersing them in acrylic. The conservators assembled the pieces with a reversible adhesive, which may be removed if additional

86. Bat God
terracotta
78 $^{7}/_{10}$ x 25 $^{3}/_{5}$ inches (200 x 65 cm)
CNCA–INAH–MEX
The Bat God is a modeled terracotta sculpture made up of five sections: the legs, a belt, a loincloth, the torso, and the head. It represents the body of a man with bat claws instead of feet and hands, and a bat's head with two pairs of fangs. Decorative elements on the figure include a protuberance on the forehead and adornments around the chin. The figure wears a necklace of three bells with human bones as clappers. The piece was finished with a thin coat of iron oxide. The sculpture probably represents a vampire bat (Desmodus rotundus).

87. The pieces of the Bat God were arranged before reassembly.

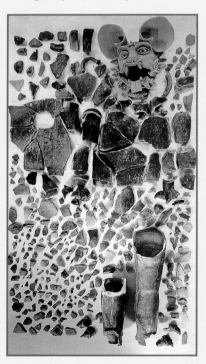

88. Xipe Totec
terracotta
29 ⁹/₁₀ x 26 inches
(76x 66 cm)
CNCA–INAH–MEX

Xipe Totec was the patron deity of goldworkers and one of the most important gods in the Aztec pantheon. A yearly ritual was held in his honor, at the end of which sacrificial victims were flayed and the skins of their bodies and faces were worn by impersonators of the god. The time of year dedicated to Xipe Totec coincided with the spring equinox, the dividing line between the dry and rainy seasons.

Like the Bat God, this figure of Xipe Totec was made in separate sections that were splattered with black paint before they were fired.

89., 90. Conservator María de la Luz Rodríquez works on restoration of the Bat God.

fragments are found. Empty spaces in the figure were filled with new material. The final steps were to add color to conceal the seams and newly created fragments, and to construct an internal metal structure to hold the sculpture together and allow it to stand on a base.

The magnificent anthropomorphic sculpture of the Bat God is one of very few known cases of a human portrayed with a bat's head, hands, and feet. The cult of the Bat God began in Mesoamerica as early as 100 B.C. At that time, the cult was especially strong among the Zapotecs of the Oaxaca region of southwestern Mexico. Later, the Mixtecs (also from Oaxaca) adopted this god and named him Tlacatzinacantli. The vampire bat, identified with night, blood sacrifice, and death, was one of the animals worshiped in the Prehispanic world. The Aztecs often depicted the bat accompanied by insects such as centipedes and spiders, and birds such as owls, creatures also associated with night and death.

When these two figures were photographed at the restoration laboratory in Churubusco, the restoration of the Bat God was nearly complete. The restoration of Xipe Totec, however, is still in progress. The torso of the reassembled figure wears armor. Bows, the symbol of Xipe, appear as a nose ornament and as decorations on the arms.

Excavations revealed that the Templo Mayor was constructed in seven stages, beginning with the simple mud and reed hut built in honor of Huitzilopochtli in 1325 when Tenochtitlan was founded. From the first primitive building, the Templo Mayor grew enormously both in size and elaboration, resulting in the magnificent structure seen by the Spanish in 1519.

The Templo Mayor was enlarged through the years for several reasons. At times the unstable lake bed on which it was built and occasional floods required that the temple's base be raised and enlarged. Most often, however, enlargements were made by the succession of powerful Aztec rulers who enhanced the Templo Mayor to celebrate their own coronations, to honor the gods, and to validate the power of the Aztec empire. The most spectacular expansions of the Templo Mayor occurred under Moctezuma I in 1454 and Axayacatl in 1469, when spectacular art and architectural elements were added.

The final stage of the Templo Mayor, the largest and most elaborate, was the temple that so astounded the Spanish conquerors. Eventually, the stones from this temple and other buildings in the sacred precinct were used to build the colonial metropolis that became Mexico City.

91. Cut-away Model of Templo Mayor CNCA–INAH–MEX, Museo del Templo Mayor, Mexico City

The Templo Mayor was constructed in seven stages, with new, larger stages enclosing smaller, older stages.

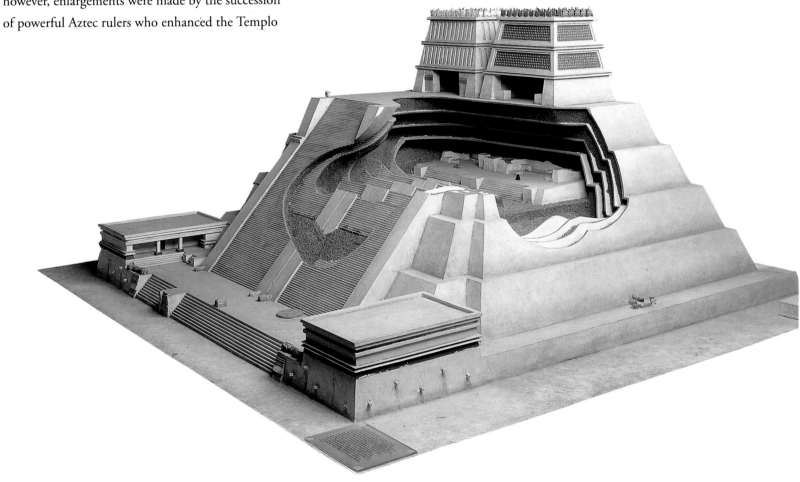

92. Huehueteotl
basalt
26 x 22 ¹/₂ x 22 inches (66 x 57.3 x 56 cm)
CNCA–INAH–MEX, Museo del Templo
Mayor, Mexico City

This crouching, cross-legged statue of Huehueteotl wears a three-stranded bead necklace and plain round earrings. Faces of demons are carved at his knees and elbows. He wears a mask around his eyes; two fangs protrude from the corners of his mouth. The circular brazier on the top of his head is decorated with bars and "eyes" along the band, and waves and snail shells on the top.

A number of magnificent stone sculptures were discovered at the Templo Mayor. Among them was a statue of Huehueteotl, the Old God, who lived at the center of the earth and held the universe in balance.

Mother of the gods, father of the gods,
The old god, lying in the navel of the
 earth,
enclosed in a turquoise chamber.
He who is in the waters that are the color
 of the blue bird,
He who is wrapped in clouds,
The old god, He who lives in the shadow
 of the land of the dead,
Lord of fire and lord of the year.[41]

This statue was carved in the style of Teotihuacan, a civilization that disappeared 500 years before the Aztecs arrived in the Valley of Mexico. By making this statue in the Teotihuacan style, the Aztec artist showed great respect and reverence for the ancient city where the Aztecs believed their own world, the Fifth Sun, was born.

The statue was discovered north of the Templo Mayor near the Red Temple, which itself was modeled after temples from Teotihuacan. The statue, dating from about A.D. 1500, was recovered from Stage VI of the Templo Mayor.

Immense ceramic braziers for burning incense were displayed in front of the temples dedicated to Tlaloc and Huitzilopochtli. Braziers on the Huitzilopochtli side were decorated with simple large bows; those on the Tlaloc side were adorned with the face of the rain god himself.

93. Weeping Tlaloc
ceramic with white stucco
24, diameter 27 ¹/₅ inches
(61, diameter 69 cm)
CNCA–INAH–MEX, Museo del Templo Mayor, Mexico City

This ceramic brazier finished with white stucco is decorated with a three-dimensional face of Tlaloc. This representation of the rain god is unique; it shows tears flowing from his eyes. The Aztecs believed that the tears of children were one of the most precious gifts to offer to this god, who brought the rains and ensured the successful growth of crops.

This brazier is one of six similar pieces that were found inside the Precinct of the Eagles adjacent to the Templo Mayor.

94. Giant Conch Shell
andesite
20 x 39 ⁴/₅ x 29 ¹/₂ inches
(51 x 101 x 75 cm)
CNCA–INAH–MEX, Museo del Templo
Mayor, Mexico City

This beautiful stone sculpture is one of
three almost identical pieces found in the
courtyard east of the Templo Mayor.
The shell represents the conch,
Strombus gigas, a species that
was once abundant in the
Gulf of Mexico.

For the Aztecs, as for many other
Mesoamerican cultures, the
conch was a symbol of life. It
was compared to the uterus, and
thus to fertility and birth. In this
sculpture, the gently flowing lines
carved into the shell create the illusion
of life's constant movement.

Archaeologists found many precious offerings dedicated to Tlaloc and Huitzilopochtli buried within the Templo Mayor. More than 100 separate offerings, containing more than 7,000 objects, were discovered. The greatest number of offerings were found between Stages IV and V, and date from 1440 to 1469, a period of great military expansion. Some of the objects were made by the Aztecs, but many came to Tenochtitlan from tribute-paying regions of the empire. Other items were antiques, originating in ancient cultures such as the Olmec and Teotihuacan. The offerings also contained many animal and plant remains.

The artifacts in the offerings symbolized the role of the Templo Mayor as the sacred and secular center of the Aztec world. Items representing water, such as greenstone beads, shells, mother-of-pearl ornaments, and bones of aquatic animals, reflect the role of Tlaloc as provider of sustenance for humans. Items such as sacrificial knives, weapons, and skulls relate to Huitzilopochtli as provider of sustenance for the empire itself in the form of sacrificial blood and the wealth of conquest.

Various kinds of greenstone, including jade, were traditionally connected with Tlaloc. The stone's blue-green color was reminiscent of water, the precious substance that provided food for the Aztec world. Throughout the prehistory of Mesoamerica, greenstone was the most valuable medium—even more so than gold—for ritual and status objects. Items such as this statue of Tlaloc, carved from a solid piece of greenstone, and miniature fish were found in offerings dedicated to Tlaloc.

The complete skeleton of a puma with a greenstone bead in its mouth was found in Chamber II dedicated to Tlaloc. Pumas, because of their swimming ability and practice of lying in wait for their prey near water at dusk, often were associated with the rain god.

95. *Tlaloc*
greenstone with inlays of pyrite and shell
12 1/5 x 7 7/10 x 6 3/10 inches
(31 x 19.5 x 16 cm)
CNCA–INAH–MEX, Museo del Templo Mayor, Mexico City

This magnificent sculpture of Tlaloc in a seated position was carved from a single block of greenstone, a material that the Aztecs thought was even more valuable than gold. The figure was found inside Chamber II of the Templo Mayor, one of the richest offerings dedicated to the god of rain.

96. *Fish*
greenstone
1 1/5 x 1 2/5 x 6 1/10 inches (3 x 3.6 x 15.6 cm)
CNCA–INAH–MEX, Museo del Templo Mayor, Mexico City

This beautifully carved and polished greenstone fish was found inside a stone box that was carved to represent Tlaloc's body. The piece is from Offering 41 of the Templo Mayor.

97. Puma with Greenstone Bead
bone, greenstone
bead: 1 ³/₅, diameter 2 ¹/₅ inches
(4.1, diameter 5.7 cm)
CNCA–INAH–MEX, Museo del Templo
Mayor, Mexico City

The complete skeleton of a puma with a greenstone bead in its mouth was found in Chamber II dedicated to Tlaloc. As part of a complicated funerary ritual, the Aztecs prepared the dead for the afterlife by placing a bead inside their mouths. If the dead person was a noble, the bead was made of fine greenstone; a commoner was buried with a bead of obsidian or speckled stone. Written sources frequently refer to greenstone as a symbol of the heart. It may have functioned as money so the dead person could pay his or her way during the journey to the underworld.

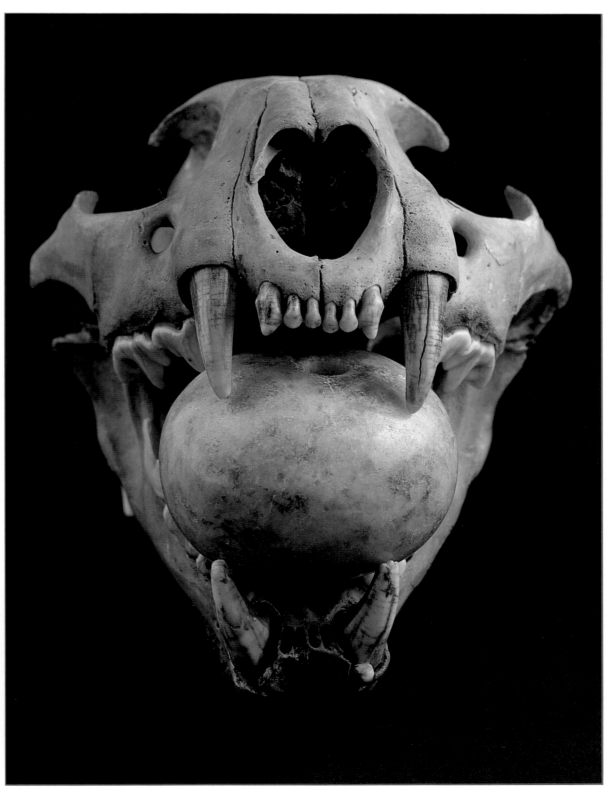

98. Vessel with Lid
ceramic and polychrome
vessel: 17 $^7/_{10}$ x 14 $^2/_5$ x 13 $^3/_5$ inches
(45.5 x 36.5 x 34.5 cm)
lid: 2 $^1/_5$ diameter 11 $^3/_5$ inches
(5.5, diameter 29.5 cm)
CNCA–INAH–MEX, Museo del Templo
Mayor, Mexico City

This magnificent Cholula ware vessel
shows Chicomecoatl, the goddess of our
sustenance, on this side. Tlaloc is on the
other side. The painted lid shows Tlaloc
with his arms outstretched as if scattering
water from a pot.

When found in Chamber III as one of
a pair, this vessel contained more than
3,000 greenstone beads. The skeleton of
a jaguar with a flint knife in its mouth
was found lying between the two vessels.
This offering also contained a variety of
masks, shells, pieces of coral, and musical
instruments.

99. Personified Sacrificial Knives
silex with overlays of obsidian and turquoise
7 x 2 ²/5 inches average (18 x 6 cm)
CNCA–INAH–MEX, Museo del Templo
Mayor, Mexico City

These personified flint knives with faces
on both sides were symbolic of sacrifice.
They are decorated with applied pieces
of turquoise, obsidian, and shell
arranged as teeth and eyes on painted
blades. The knives were recovered
from Offering 52 on the Huitzilopochtli
side of the Templo Mayor.

Offerings to Huitzilopochtli, the Aztec god of war and the sun, contained a variety of items symbolic of his power and strength. The offerings included symbols of human sacrifice such as braziers with knotted bows, knives, and human skulls as well as many objects from tribute-paying regions of the Aztec empire.

Unlike the offerings dedicated to Tlaloc, those to Huitzilopochtli contained no images of the god. Spanish chroniclers recorded that images of Huitzilopochtli often were made of amaranth dough and then decorated with clothing, jewels, and weapons.

Many of the items contained in the Templo Mayor offerings were not made by the Aztecs; they were brought to Tenochtitlan from far corners of the Aztec empire. Greenstone masks and figures from Guerrero, polychrome pottery from Puebla, gold from the Mixteca region, and shells from both east and west coasts were discovered. These artifacts are symbolic of Aztec conquest and dominance over distant realms and people.

100. Deer Head
alabaster
4 x 1 ³/₁₀ x ¹/₅ inches (10.5 x 3.4 x 2 cm)
CNCA–INAH–MEX, Museo del Templo Mayor, Mexico City

In ancient Mesoamerica, the deer symbolized the sun and fire. This beautifully carved miniature scepter of a deer head was found in an offering contained in the rubble beneath the floor on the northwest corner of the Templo Mayor's main platform. Similar figures were found in association with miniature scepters that symbolized water and fertility.

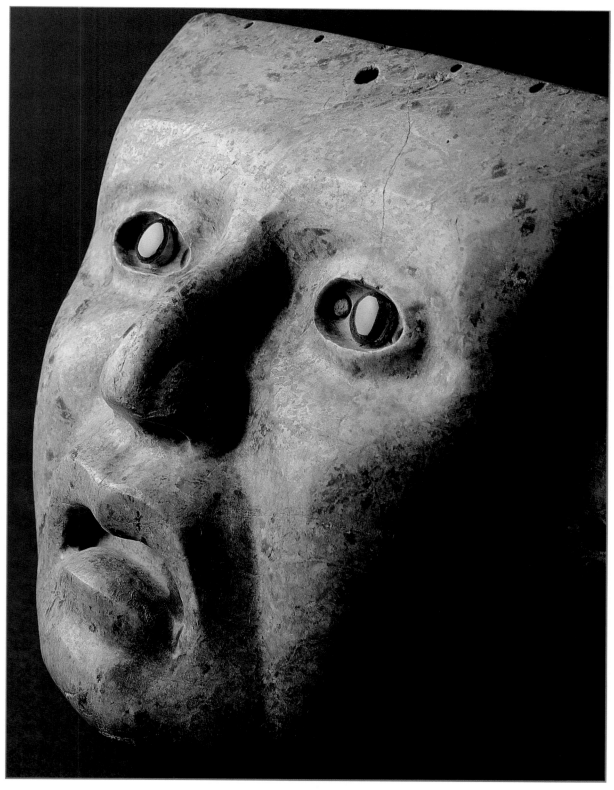

101. *Teotihuacan Mask*
greenstone and obsidian
3 ¹/₅ x 9 ¹/₅ x 8 inches (9 x 24.2 x 20.4 cm)
CNCA–INAH–MEX, Museo del Templo
Mayor, Mexico City

*This beautiful greenstone mask with
highly-polished obsidian eyes was made
in Teotihuacan about 1,000 years before
it was buried, as a valued heirloom, at
the Templo Mayor. It was recovered
from Offering 20 on the east side of the
Templo Mayor where the Tlaloc and
Huitzilopochtli sides of the temple met.*

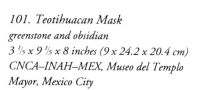

The Conquest:
An Encounter of Two Worlds

One of the most dramatic events in history was the encounter of the Old and New Worlds in the Americas during the late fifteenth and early sixteenth centuries. Of all these events, the meeting between the forces of Spanish Captain Hernán Cortés and the Aztecs under Moctezuma II is the most astounding.

On February 18, 1519, Hernán Cortés set sail from Cuba to search for gold, glory, and souls. He was accompanied by 500 soldiers, 50 sailors, 200 Cuban bearers, several African servants, and a few Indian women. Also on board his 11 ships were 16 horses, 14 pieces of artillery, supplies of food, and trinkets and clothing for trading. Speaking to his men, Cortés laid out his dream,

> I offer you great rewards, although they will be wrapped about with great hardships. . . . And if you do not abandon me, as I shall not abandon you, I shall make you in a very short time the richest of all men who have crossed the seas. . . . You are few, but such is your spirit that no effort or force of Indians will prevail against you.[42]

Cortés first landed in Mexico on the Yucatan Peninsula and then sailed his ships up the Gulf Coast. Along the way, he heard of the power and wealth of the Aztec empire, ruled by the feared emperor Moctezuma. On Good Friday, April 18, 1519, Cortés and his men landed near the modern city of Veracruz and established a town. In July, the Spaniards began their march inland to Tenochtitlan.

From the first appearance of Cortés and his ships, Moctezuma was made aware of their presence by reports from his emissaries and spies. He was perplexed by descriptions of the strange winged towers floating on the sea, and people with white skin and beards.

Moctezuma wondered if the strangers' presence was related to a series of evil omens that had plagued the Aztecs for 10 years. Legends recorded that a great fire appeared in the night sky and burned until dawn every night for a year. The temple of Huitzilopochtli mysteriously burst into flames and could not be saved. A strange bird with a round mirror on its chest was captured and taken to Moctezuma. In the mirror he saw people dressed for battle, riding on the backs of deer. Moctezuma questioned his wise men and magicians about the meaning of these signs. No one could answer him except to say,

> "What can we say? The future has already been determined and decreed in heaven, and [Moctezuma] will behold and suffer a great mystery which must come to pass in this land. If our king wishes to know more about it, he will know soon enough, for it comes swiftly."[43]

102. Spanish soldiers arrive at Veracruz (from the Florentine Codex*).*

103. A large flame appeared in the night sky (from the Florentine Codex).

104. A bird with a mirror on its chest was taken to Moctezuma (from the Florentine Codex).

105. Spanish troops marched toward Tenochtitlan (from the Florentine Codex).

Increasingly concerned about the portent of the omens and the arrival of strangers from the sea, Moctezuma sent ambassadors to the Spanish with elaborate gifts.

The first was a disk in the shape of the sun, as big as a cartwheel and made of very fine gold . . . a marvelous thing. . . . There was another larger disk of brightly shining silver in the shape of the moon. . . . Next they brought crests of gold, plumes of rich green feathers, silver crests, some fans of the same material, models of deer in hollow gold . . . and . . . thirty loads of beautiful cotton cloth.[44]

The ambassadors also brought the sacred costume of the god Quetzalcoatl and arrayed Cortés in the magnificent garments. Cortés's arrival in Mexico on the Aztec calendar date ce acatl (One Reed) prompted Moctezuma to consider that Cortés might actually be Quetzalcoatl himself, returning, as promised in legend, to reclaim his kingdom in the year One Reed. This coincidence of the date of Cortés's arrival, coupled with the uncertainty produced by the evil omens, left Moctezuma perplexed as to Cortés's identity and purpose.

When messengers returned to Tenochtitlan, they told Moctezuma of the great "stags" ridden by the Spanish, of the enormous dogs whose yellow eyes flashed fire, and of the cannon that roared and shot a ball of stone out its entrails, shooting sparks and raining fire. Moctezuma was not sure how to treat the strange invaders: Were they gods or mortal enemies?

Cortés used the time allowed by Moctezuma's vacillation to great advantage. With his appetite for gold heightened by the extravagant gifts from the emperor, Cortés was determined to have more. Through the shrewd assistance of a young Indian woman, Doña Marina—also known as La Malinche—who became his interpreter and mistress, Cortés quickly adapted his plans to the political dissensions of the Aztec world. He convinced local officials to provide him with men and supplies for the difficult inland journey and on August 16, Cortés, his soldiers, 15 horses, and a group of Indian allies departed for Tenochtitlan.

During the long and arduous march, Cortés enlisted the aid of disgruntled leaders of Tlaxcalla, traditional enemies of the Aztecs, who had wearied of Moctezuma's ill treatment and heavy tribute demands. By the time Cortés crossed the last great mountain barrier and descended into the Valley of Mexico, his entourage consisted of several thousand Tlaxcallan warriors well equipped with food and weapons, and the 350 Spanish soldiers who survived the inland march.

On November 8, 1519, the Aztec ruler Moctezuma Xocoyotzin and Spanish Captain Hernán Cortés met on a causeway approaching the capital city of Tenochtitlan. Tens of thousands of Aztecs watched from their rooftops and canoes as the Spanish approached, dressed in their shining metal armor. It was a momentous encounter between two worlds, marked with fear, apprehension, and excitement on both sides.

Perhaps Moctezuma had become convinced by the evil omens that the Spanish were invincible; perhaps he even believed that the god Quetzalcoatl had returned. At any rate, he welcomed Cortés to Tenochtitlan with these words:

> "Our lord, you are weary. The journey has tired you, but now you have arrived on the earth. You have come to your city, [Tenochtitlan]. You have come here to sit on your throne, to sit under its canopy."[45]

106. On November 8, 1519, the Aztec ruler Moctezuma II and Spanish Captain Hernán Cortés, accompanied by his translator Doña Marina, met on a causeway leading into Tenochtitlan. Within two years of this fateful encounter, the Aztec empire fell.

The Spanish soldier, Bernal Díaz del Castillo, recorded his impression of the encounter as follows:

When Cortés saw . . . that the great [Moctezuma] was approaching, he dismounted from his horse, and when he came near to [Moctezuma] each bowed deeply to the other. [Moctezuma] welcomed our Captain, and Cortés, speaking through Doña Marina, answered by wishing him very good health. Cortés . . . offered [Moctezuma] his right hand, but [Moctezuma] refused it and extended his own. Then Cortés brought out a necklace . . . made of . . . elaborately worked and coloured glass beads . . . strung on a gold cord. . . . This he hung round the great [Moctezuma's] neck, and as he did so attempted to embrace him. But the great princes who stood around [Moctezuma] grasped Cortés' arm to prevent him, for they considered this an indignity.[46]

The Spanish, incredibly, became the guests of Moctezuma. They were housed in the palace of the emperor's deceased father, which they quickly plundered of its treasures. The Spanish took Moctezuma hostage, yet he continued to supply the invaders with food and was submissive to them. Moctezuma's behavior angered the populace of Tenochtitlan.

At some point during the battle Moctezuma was killed, perhaps by his own people. He was succeeded by his brother, Cuitlahuac. The Spaniards fled over the mountains to Tlaxcalla, the home of their most loyal allies. The Aztecs thought their enemies had departed for good and would never return; the city returned to its normal daily and ceremonial routine. But the short respite quickly ended when a great plague of smallpox spread rapidly through the city. The inhabitants of the Americas had no immunity to this disease brought by the Spanish, which killed many thousands of people, one of them the new Aztec ruler.

107. Fighting during la Noche Triste *(from the* Florentine Codex*).*

108. Moctezuma died during the fighting (from the Florentine Codex*).*

109. Plagues of smallpox ravaged the Aztecs (from the Florentine Codex*).*

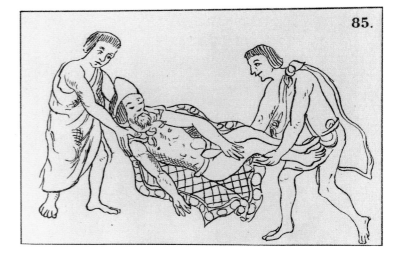

When the Spanish treacherously massacred a large group of warriors and dancers during a celebration in honor of Huitzilopochtli, the Aztecs finally turned on the Spanish soldiers. On the night of July 10, 1520, eight months after the Spanish had entered the city, the Aztecs drove them from Tenochtitlan in a furious battle. Spanish losses were so great, the battle came to be known as the Night of Sorrow, *la Noche Triste.*

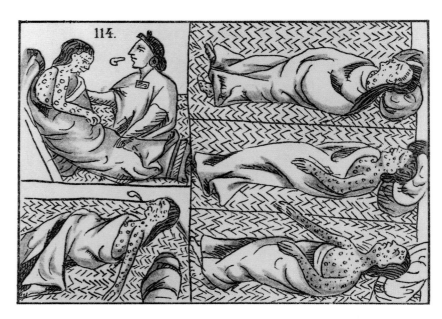

117.

110. Hand-to-hand fighting on the causeways was fierce (from the Florentine Codex).

The illness was so dreadful that no one could walk or move. The sick were so utterly helpless that they could only lie on their beds like corpses, unable to move their limbs or even their heads. They could not lie face down or roll from one side to the other. If they did move their bodies they screamed in pain.

A great many died from this plague, and many others died of hunger. They could not get up to search for food, and everyone else was too sick to care for them, so they starved to death in their beds.[47]

On April 28, 1521, the Spanish marched back to Tenochtitlan with large forces of Indian allies and 900 soldiers, many of them new recruits from Spain and the Indies. On May 31, 1521, Cortés began his final siege of the city. From the edges of the lake the Spanish launched their major weapon in the battle for Tenochtitlan—a fleet of brigantines small enough to navigate the shallow waters of the Valley. These small ships had been constructed by Indian labor under the supervision of the Spanish and had been carried across the mountain passes. Armed with cannon, the ships proved an invincible weapon against the canoes of Tenochtitlan's flotilla. An Aztec eyewitness reported,

> The cannons were fired into the thick of the flotilla, wherever the canoes were crowded closest together. Many of our warriors were killed outright; others drowned because they were too crippled by their wounds to swim away. The water was red with the blood of the dead and the dying.[48]

111. Spanish brigantines assault the city (from the Florentine Codex).

120.

A major Spanish objective was to drive the Aztec canoes and warriors back into Tenochtitlan so that the canals could be filled in, and horsemen and soldiers could be brought into the city from the mainland. With the objective finally accomplished, Spanish soldiers and cavalry poured into the city. Over and over again the Spaniards were driven back by the Aztec warriors. The siege of the capital lasted 75 days, causing great suffering to the people of Tenochtitlan.

Nothing can compare with the horrors of
that siege and the agonies of the starving.
We were so weakened by hunger that, little
by little, the enemy forced us to retreat.
Little by little they forced us to the wall.[49]

The final battle for Tenochtitlan was fought in
the great marketplace of Tlatelolco. There
Cuauhtemoc, the last Aztec ruler, gathered with
his nobles and warriors and, according to legend,
assisted even by the women, made his last stand for
the city. But the forces of the Spanish and their
thousands of Indian allies were too powerful. Streets
were lined with bodies of the dead and wounded.
Survivors attempted to flee. Entire areas of the city
were looted and demolished, leaving only piles of
rubble behind. Temples were burned and
destroyed. The end came on August 13, 1521.
Of the approximate 300,000 Aztec defenders of
Tenochtitlan, only about 60,000 survived.

> Broken spears lie in the roads;
>
> we have torn our hair in our grief.
>
> The houses are roofless now, and their walls
>
> are red with blood.
>
> . . . .
>
> We have pounded our hands in despair
>
> against the adobe walls,
>
> for our inheritance, our city, is lost
>   and dead.
>
> The shields of our warriors were its defense,
>
> but they could not save it.[50]

The Aztec empire had fallen. The glorious city of
Tenochtitlan was destroyed. Neither the New World
nor the Old would ever be the same again. In less
than two years after the arrival of Cortés, the mighty
Aztec capital of Tenochtitlan was destroyed. Within
10 years, most of Mexico—or New Spain as it was
called by the Spanish—was under Spanish control.

Soon Spanish adventurers, priests, bureaucrats,
and soldiers flocked to New Spain to look for fame
and fortune and to convert souls. A few came to
make Mexico their home; others came to convert
the Indians to Catholicism. Most, however, came
simply to pillage the wealth of the new land. For
almost 300 years the Aztecs and other indigenous
peoples lay under the colonial yoke of Spain. In the
early 1800s, the war of independence finally broke
the bonds that tied New Spain to Europe. Mexico
rose as a new country, a nation that blended the
genes and customs of Old and New Worlds in a
tradition unique to the Americas.

*112. The final battle for Tenochtitlan
ended with the burning of the temple at
Tlatelolco (from the* Florentine Codex*).*

Notes

1. *Códice Matritense de la Real Academia*, VIII, fol. 116,r., in Miguel León-Portilla, *Aztec Thought and Culture*, trans. J. E. Davis, (Norman, 1963), p. 172.

2. Bernal Díaz del Castillo, *The Conquest of New Spain*, trans. J. M. Cohen, (Baltimore, 1963), pp. 224-25.

3. Domingo Chimalpain Cuauhtlehuanitzin, *Memorial Breve de la fundación de la ciudad de Culhuacán, apud* Lehmann, *Die Geschichte*, 111, in León-Portilla, *Aztec Thought and Culture*, p. 158.

4. Eduardo Matos Moctezuma, *The Great Temple of the Aztecs: Treasures of Tenochtitlan*, trans. D. Heyden, (London, 1988), p. 43.

5. Fray Diego Durán, *Book of the Gods and Rites of the Ancient Calendar*, trans. and ed. F. Horcasitas and D. Heyden, (Norman, 1971), p. 78.

6. *Cantares Mexicanos*, fol. 19 v.–20 r. in Miguel León-Portilla, *Pre-Columbian Literatures of Mexico*, trans. G. Lobanov, (Norman, 1969), p. 87.

7. Díaz del Castillo, *The Conquest of New Spain*, p. 214.

8. Fray Bernardino de Sahagún, *Florentine Codex: General History of the Things of New Spain*, trans. A. J. O. Anderson and C. E. Dibble (Salt Lake City and Santa Fe, 1950–1982), Book 8, p. 37

9. Sahagún, *Florentine Codex*, Book 5, p. 184.

10. Jacques Soustelle, *The Daily Life of the Aztecs on the Eve of the Spanish Conquest*, trans. P. O'Brian, (Harmondsworth, 1961), p. 238.

11. Manuscript of 1558, fol. 75–76, in León-Portilla, *Pre-Columbian Literatures of Mexico*, p. 40.

12. Sahagún, *Florentine Codex*, Book 10, p. 30.

13. Sahagún, *Florentine Codex*, Book 6, pp. 176–77.

14. Sahagún, *Florentine Codex*, Book 6, p. 129.

15. Sahagún, *Florentine Codex*, Book 6, p. 130.

16. *MSS Romances de los Señores de la Nueva España*, fol. 2 r., in León-Portilla, *Pre-Columbian Literatures of Mexico*, p. 80.

17. Díaz del Castillo, *The Conquest of New Spain*, pp. 234–35.

18. Sahagún, *Florentine Codex*, Book 10, p. 15.

19. *Códice Matritense de la Real Academia*, VIII, fols. 172, v. and 176, r., in León-Portilla, *Aztec Thought and Culture*, p. 168.

20. *Códice Matritense del Real Palacio*, fol. 132 v.–134 v., in León-Portilla, *Pre-Columbian Literatures of Mexico*, p. 42.

21. Fray Diego Durán, *The Aztecs: The History of the Indies of New Spain*, trans. D. Heyden and F. Horcasitas, (New York, 1964), pp. 131–32.

22. Díaz del Castillo, *The Conquest of New Spain*, pp. 225–27.

23. *Cantares Mexicanos*, fol. 19 v.–20 r., in León-Portilla, *Pre-Columbian Literatures of Mexico*, pp. 86–87.

24. Durán, *Book of the Gods and Rites*, p. 316.

25. Durán, *Book of the Gods and Rites*, p. 315.

26. Durán, *Book of the Gods and Rites*, p. 304.

27. *Colección de Cantares Mexicanos*, ed. by Antonio Peñafiel, fol. 17,r., in León-Portilla, *Aztec Thought and Culture*, p. 7.

28. *Códice Matritense de la Real Academia*, VIII, fol. 192,r., in León-Portilla, *Aztec Thought and Culture*, p. 23.

29. Lehmann (ed.), *Colloquies and Christian Doctrine*, pp. 100–106, in León-Portilla, *Aztec Thought and Culture*, p. 64.

30. Patricia de Fuentes, *The Conquistadors*, (New York, 1963), p. 164.

31. Sahagún, *Florentine Codex*, Book 2, p. 216.

32. *Manuscript of 1588*, also known as *Legend of the Suns*, fol. 77. included as an appendix to the text of Anales de Cuauhtitlán, in León-Portilla, *Pre-Columbian Literatures of Mexico*, p. 37.

33. Lehmann (ed.), *Colloquies and Christian Doctrine*, pp. 100–106, in León-Portilla, *Aztec Thought and Culture*, p. 64.

34. Sahagún, *Florentine Codex*, Book 2, pp. 66–68.

35. Sahagún, *Florentine Codex*, Book 1, p. 7.

36. Angel María Garibay K. (ed.), *Viente Himnos Sacros de los Nahuas*, 31, in León-Portilla, *Aztec Thought and Culture*, p. 161.

37. Sahagún, quoted in E. W. Weismann, *Mexico in Sculpture 1521–1821*, p. 33, in Inga Clendinnen, *Aztecs*, (Cambridge, 1991), p. 226.

38. Eduardo Matos Moctezuma, *The Great Temple of the Aztecs*, p. 65.

39. Johanna Broda, Davíd Carrasco, and Eduardo Matos Moctezuma, *The Great Temple of Tenochtitlan: Center and Periphery in the Aztec World*, (Berkeley, 1987), pp. 49-55.

40. *Florentine Codex*, Book III, Chapter I, in León-Portilla, *Pre-Columbian Literatures of Mexico*, p. 48.

41. Eduardo Matos Moctezuma, *Treasures of the Great Temple*, (La Jolla, 1990), p. 115.

42. Francisco Lopez de Gomara, Cortez: *The Life of the Conqueror by His Secretary*, trans. and ed. L. B. Simpson, (Berkeley, 1964), p. 25.

43. Miguel León-Portilla, *The Broken Spears*, trans. L. Kemp, (Boston, 1962), pp. 14-15.

44. Díaz del Castillo, *The Conquest of New Spain*, p. 93.

45. León-Portilla, *The Broken Spears*, p. 64.

46. Díaz del Castillo, *The Conquest of New Spain*, pp. 217-218.

47. León-Portilla, *The Broken Spears*, p. 93.

48. León-Portilla, *The Broken Spears*, p. 96.

49. León-Portilla, *The Broken Spears*, p. 109.

50. León-Portilla, *The Broken Spears*, pp. 137-138.

Glossary

Acamapichtli (A-ka-ma-PEECH-tlee)—"Handful of Reeds," first Aztec ruler from 1372–1391.

amaranth—native plant of the Americas; grown by Aztecs as source of protein.

atolli (a-TO-lee)—A corn gruel often served sweetened with honey or seasoned with fruit or chocolate.

autosacrifice—practice of drawing one's own blood by piercing the skin with sharp objects such as maguey cactus spines.

Axayacatl (A-sha-YA-katl)—"Water Face," sixth Aztec ruler from 1468–1481.

Aztec—"people of Aztlan," one of several groups of Indians of central Mexico that shared a similar language and customs during the two centuries prior to the Spanish conquest.

Aztlan—"Place of the Herons," mythic island homeland of the Aztecs located northwest of the Valley of Mexico.

Bat God—also called Tlacatzinacantli, god associated with death.

cacao—chocolate. Beans were ground and used as a beverage; whole beans were used as currency.

calmecac (kal-ME-kak)—school reserved for young men of nobility, associated with temples and priests.

calpulli (kal-PO-lee)—basic social, economic, and religious unit of Aztec society.

causeway—strip of land built over water; three connected Tenochtitlan to the mainland.

Chalchiuhtlicue (Chal-chee-uh-TLEE-kwe)—"She of the Jade Skirt," goddess of water, Tlaloc's consort.

Chichimeca (Chee-chee-ME-ka)—early groups of nomadic hunter-gatherers living in the northern deserts of Mexico.

Chicomecoatl (Chee-ko-ma-KO-atl)—"Goddess of Our Sustenance," also known as "Seven Serpents."

Chicomoztoc (Chee-ko-MOS-tok)—"Seven Caves," area from which the early Aztec tribes began their migration.

chinampas (chee-NAM-paz)—plots of land built in shallow lakebeds; used to increase agricultural land.

Cholula (Cho-LOO-la)—city in the present-day state of Puebla, east of Tenochtitlan; area where fine polychrome pottery was made.

cihuateteo (see-wa-te-TAY-o) (sing. cihuateotl)—spirits of women who died in childbirth; they carried the sun from its zenith to the sunset.

Coatepec (Ko-ah-TAY-pec)—"Hill of the Serpent," location near Tula where Huitzilopochtli was born as the Aztec's supreme god, where he defeated his sister Coyolxauhqui (the moon) and his 400 brothers (the stars).

Coatlicue (Co-at-LEE-kwa)—"She of the Serpent Skirt," mother goddess, mother of Huitzilopochtli, Coyolxauhqui, and of the four hundred southerners.

codex—an ancient handwritten document recorded by specially trained scribes; an official record written in pictures.

comitl (KO-mitl)—a round, flat griddle used for baking tortillas, traditionally placed over three hearth stones.

copal—incense made from the resin of conifer trees.

Cortés, Hernán—leader of the Spanish army that conquered the Aztecs.

Coyolxauhqui (Ko-yol-sha-UH-kee)—"Bells on Her Cheeks," goddess of the moon, defeated and dismembered by her brother, Huitzilopochtli, at Coatepec.

Cuauhtemoc (Kwa-uh-TE-mok)—last Aztec ruler, 1520–1525.

cuicacalli (kwee-ka-KA-lee)—"house of song," local temple school attended by boys and girls between ages 12 and 15.

Cuitlahuac (Kwee-TLA-wak)—Aztec ruler who succeeded Moctezuma II, in 1520.

Díaz del Castillo, Bernal—Spanish chronicler and soldier in Cortés's army.

Durán, Fray Diego—Spanish friar; author of *Codex Durán*.

Eagle Warrior—an elite military order of the nobility.

Ehecatl (A-HA-katl)—"God of the Wind," a personality of Quetzalcoatl.

Fifth Sun—the Aztecs' world.

greenstone—blue-green stone valued for ritual and status objects.

Huehueteotl (Way-way-TA-otl)—the "Old God," an aspect of Xiuhtecuhtli, the old god of fire.

huictli (WEEK-tli)—a simple pointed stick used to plant and cultivate crops.

Huitzilopochtli (Wee-tsee-lo-POCH-tlee)—patron god of the Aztecs, war god, sun god, god to whom warriors dedicated their services; required human blood and hearts for nourishment.

Itzcoatl (Eets-KO-atl)—"Obsidian Serpent," fourth Aztec ruler from 1426–1440.

Jaguar Warrior—an elite military order of the nobility.

La Malinche—interpreter for Cortés and his mistress, also known as Doña Marina.

la Noche Triste—"Night of Sorrow," battle in which the Aztecs drove the Spanish from Tenochtitlan, July 10, 1520.

Lake Texcoco (Tesh-KO-ko)—the lake in which the island city of Tenochtitlan was founded.

macehualtin (ma-se-WAL-teen) (sing. macehualli)—common people, free men and women who belonged to a calpulli and formed the labor forces of the Aztec empire; men were trained as warriors.

maguey—spiny-leaved cactus.

mayeque (ma-YE-ke)—landless commoners who farmed the lands of the nobles; were not members of a calpulli; class below macehualtin.

Mesoamerica—geographic area that includes Mexico and much of Central America; during the Prehispanic period, the population shared many cultural traits.

metlatl (MAY-tlatl)—a stone on which softened corn was ground.

Mictlan (MEEK-tlan)—"Place of Darkness," where most people went after death.

Mictlantecuhtli (Mic-tlan-tee-KOO-tlee)—"Lord of Mictlan," god of death and the underworld.

Moctezuma Xocoyotzin (Mo-tek-ZU-ma Sho-ko-YO-tsin)—"Angry Lord," also known as Moctezuma II (the younger), the last great Aztec ruler from 1502–1520.

Nahuatl (Na-watl)—the language of the Aztecs.

New Fire Ceremony—a religious event held every 52 years to prevent the destruction of the Fifth Sun.

nopal cactus—type of cactus common throughout the Valley of Mexico, fermented into alcoholic beverage called pulque; type of cactus on which eagle perched—the sign foretold by Huitzilopochtli for the founding of Tenochtitlan.

Olmec (OHL-mek)—earliest known civilization of Mexico, 1500–400 B.C.

patolli (pa-TO-lee)—a game of chance similar to Parcheesi.

pipiltin (pi-PIL-teen) (sing. pilli)—lowest class of the nobility; held government, religious, and military positions.

pochtecah (poch-TE-kah) (sing. pochtecatl)—long distance traders, held intermediate position between nobles and commoners.

Quetzalcoatl (Ket-tsal-KO-atl)—"Feathered Serpent," creator god who gave the arts and maize to humans.

sacred precinct—spiritual and physical center of Tenochtitlan that contained Templo Mayor and other buildings.

Sahagún, Bernardino de—Spanish friar, author of *Florentine Codex.*

tamales—food made of ground corn and filling steamed inside corn husk, a favorite food of the Aztecs.

Tamoanchan (Ta-MUAN-chan)—place along Aztec migration route where tree broke in half and destroyed temple to Huitzilopochtli, where Aztecs separated from other groups and continued their migration alone.

Tarascans—powerful neighbors to the west whom Aztecs never conquered.

techcatl (TECH-catl)—sacrificial stone.

tecuitlatl (te-KWEE-tlatl)—green lake scum dried into bricks and tasting like cheese.

telpochcalli (tel-poch-KA-lee)—"house of youth," district school for young men of commoner background beginning at age 15.

Templo Mayor—"Great Temple," dedicated to worship of Tlaloc and Huitzilopochtli, located within the sacred precinct, symbol of the sacred and secular center of the Aztec world.

Tenochtitlan (Te-noch-TEET-lan)—"Place of the Prickly Pear Cactus Fruit," capital city of Aztec empire, founded 1325.

Teotihuacan (Te-o-tee-WA-kan)—"Place Where the Gods Were Born," large ancient city in south central Mexico built between 100 B.C. and A.D. 750.

tetecutin (te-TEK'W-teen) (sing. tecutli)—middle rank of the nobility; served as chiefs, advisors to rulers, judges, generals, or tax collectors.

Tezcatlipoca (Tes-kat-lee-PO-ka)—"Lord of the Smoking Mirror," God of Gods, god of Aztec kings, associated with theme of creation.

ticitl (TEE-ceetl)—physicians.

tlachtli (TLACH-tlee)—a popular ballgame.

tlacotin (tla-KO-tin) (sing. tlacotli)—slaves.

tlacuilo (tla-KWEE-lo)—a painter.

Tlaloc (TLA-lok)—god of rain and fertility, one of the two main Aztec deities worshiped atop the Templo Mayor.

Tlalocan (Tla-LO-kan)—"Place of Tlaloc," place of pleasure where people whose death related to water went in the afterlife.

tlameme (tla-MAY-may)—free men who hired themselves out as porters.

Tlatelolco (Tla-te-LOL-ko)—location of the great Aztec marketplace.

tlatoani (tla-to-A-nee) (sing. tlatoque)—"he who speaks," the noble ruler of a city-state or region, the highest ranking position in the social system.

Tlaxcalla (Tlash-KA-lah)—powerful neighboring city-state that the Aztecs never conquered. Tlaxcallan warriors became allies of the Spanish.

Toltec—ancient civilization of Mexico that founded city of Tula, A.D. 900–1150.

toltecah (tol-TAY-kah) (sing. toltecatl)—crafters of luxury goods, intermediate social class between nobles and commoners.

Tonacatepetl (Toh-na-ka-TAY-petl)—"Hill of Sustenance," the place where Quetzalcoatl turned himself into an ant and brought corn to humans.

Triple Alliance—military alliance of the city-states of Tenochtitlan, Texcoco, and Tlacopan in the fifteenth century.

Valley of Mexico—large inland basin surrounded by volcanic peaks located in central Mexico, where Mexico City is now located.

Xipe Totec (SHEE-pe TO-tek)—"Our Lord the Flayed One," the patron god of goldworkers, god of early spring whose ceremony included the flaying and wearing of the skin of a sacrificial victim.

Xiuhtecuhtli (She-oo-te-KOO-tlee)—"Old God of Fire," also known as "Turquoise Lord."

Xolotl (SHO-lotl)—god of twins and of the underworld, the dog, twin of Quetzalcoatl.

Photography Credits

Dimensions are given in inches followed by centimeters in parentheses. Unless otherwise specified, height precedes width precedes depth.

CNCA–INAH–MEX: Figure 87. ©DENVER MUSEUM OF NATURAL HISTORY: Figures 13, 14, 89, and 90 by Nancy K. Jenkins. SALVADOR GUIL'LIEM A., CNCA–INAH–MEX, Museo del Templo Mayor, Mexico City: Figure 85. DAVID HISER/PHOTOGRAPHERS ASPEN: Figure 81. SOPRINTENDENZA PER I BENI ARTISTICI E STORICI, FLORENCE, Photograph by Dagli Orti Alfredo: p. viii. MICHEL ZABÉ: front cover; back cover; front flap; back flap; inside front cover; inside back cover; Figures 7, 10, 12 (2), 15, 18, 21 (2), 23 (2), 25, 26, 28, 37, 38, 39, 40, 48, 49, 54, 57, 59, 60, 64, 66, 68, 69 (2), 70, 73, 74, 76, 77, 78, 79, 82, 83, 84, 86, 88, 91, 92, 93, 94, 95, 96, 97, 98, 99, 100, 101.

Illustration Credits

©THOMAS HALLER BUCHANAN: Figures 11, 24, 50, 61. *CODEX BORBONICUS*, Bibliothèque de l'Assemblee Nationale, Paris: Figures 16, fol. 23 (detail); 20, fol. 5 (detail).; 22, fol. 7 (detail); 44, fol. 22 (detail); 63, fol. 34 (detail); 71, fol. 14 (detail); 75, fol. 10 (detail). *CODEX IXTLILXOCHITL*, Bibliothèque Nationale, Paris: Figures 45, fol. 108r; 46, fol. 105r.; 80, fol. 112v. *CODEX MAGLIABECCHIANO*, Biblioteca Nazionale Centrale, Florence: Figures 52, fol. 68; 53, fol. 48. *CODEX MENDOZA*, ms. Arch. Seld. a.1., The Bodleian Library, Oxford: Figures 2. fol. 15v. (detail); 5, fol. 2r.; 8, fol. 69r. (detail); 31, fol. 57r (detail); 32, fol. 60r (detail); 33, fol. 60r (detail); 34, fol. 60r (detail); 35, fol. 61r (detail); 36, fol. 71r (detail); 42, fol. 47r.; 47, fol. 68r (detail); 51, fol. 64r (detail); 56, fol. 63r (detail); 88, fol. 67r (detail). ©DENVER MUSEUM OF NATURAL HISTORY: Figures 3 and 4, redrawn from the *Codex Boturini* by R. Farrington; Map 6, Gail Kohler Opsahl. *FLORENTINE CODEX*, Biblioteca Medicea Laurenziana, Florence: Figures 17, Book 4, fol. 173; 19, Book 4, fol. 172; 27, Book 9, fol. 63; 29, Book 11, fol. 157; 30, Book 11, fol. 147; 41, Book 9, fol. 8; 43, Book 8, fol. 34; 58, Book 8, fol. 30; 62, Book 7, fol. 20; 65, Book 2, fol. 17; 67, Book 7, fol. 21; 72, Book 2, fol. 122. Drawings by Francisco del Paso y Troncoso as reproduced in the *FLORENTINE CODEX: THE GENERAL HISTORY OF THE THINGS OF NEW SPAIN*, by Bernardino de Sahagún, translated by Charles E. Dibble and Arthur J. O. Anderson, Book 12, Santa Fe and Salt Lake City, School of American Research and the University of Utah: Figures 102, 103, 104, 105, 107, 108, 109, 110, 111, 112. ©1992 SCOTT GENTLING, Fort Worth: pp. iv–v, vi. ©1992 STUART GENTLING, Fort Worth: pp. ii–iii. KEITH HENDERSON, illustrator, *The Conquest of Mexico*, by W. H. Prescott, New York: Henry Holt and Company, 1922: Figure 55. NEWBERRY LIBRARY, Chicago: Figure 9. NED M. SEIDLER, © National Geographic Society: Figures 81 (overlay), 106.

Selected Bibliography

Anawalt, Patricia R. *Indian Clothing Before Cortez.* Norman: University of Oklahoma Press, 1981.

Aveni, Anthony. *Skywatchers of Ancient Mexico.* Austin: University of Texas Press, 1980.

Berdan, Frances F. *The Aztecs of Central Mexico: An Imperial Society.* New York: Holt, Rhinehart and Winston, 1982.

_____. *The Aztecs.* New York and Philadelphia: Chelsea House, 1989.

_____, and Patricia R. Anawalt. *Codex Mendoza.* Berkeley: University of California Press, 1992.

Boone, Elizabeth, ed. *The Art and Iconography of Late Preclassic Mexico.* Washington D.C.: Dumbarton Oaks, 1982.

_____, ed. *The Aztec Templo Mayor.* Washington D.C.: Dumbarton Oaks, 1987.

_____, ed. *Ritual Human Sacrifice in Mesoamerica.* Washington D.C.: Dumbarton Oaks, 1984.

Broda, Johanna, Davíd Carrasco, and Eduardo Matos Moctezuma. *The Great Temple of Tenochtitlan: Center and Periphery in the Aztec World.* Berkeley, Los Angeles, and London: University of California Press, 1987.

Brotherston, Gordon, ed. *Image of the New World: The American Continent Portrayed in Native Texts.* Translated by Gordon Brotherston and Ed Dorn. London: Thames and Hudson, 1979.

Carrasco, Davíd. *Religions of Mesoamerica: Cosmovision and Ceremonial Centers.* San Francisco: Harper and Row, 1990.

_____, ed. *To Change Place: Aztec Ceremonial Landscapes.* Boulder: University Press of Colorado, 1991.

Caso, Alfonso. *The Aztecs: People of the Sun.* Translated by Lowell Durham. Norman: University of Oklahoma Press, 1958.

Clendinnen, Inga. *Aztecs.* New York: Cambridge University Press, 1991.

Codex Borbonicus: Bibliotheque de l'Assemblee Nationale, Paris (Y120). Facsimile. Ausgabe de Codex im Original format. Edited by Karl Nowotny. Vollstandige. Graz: Akademische Druk-u. Verlagsanstalt, 1974.

Codex Boturini. Mexico City: Librería Anticuaria, 1944.

Codex Magliabecchiano. Edited by Elizabeth Hill Boone and Zelia Nuttall. Berkeley: University of California Press, 1983.

Codex Mendoza (1541). Translated and edited by James Cooper Clark. London: Waterlow and Sons, 1938.

Coe, Michael D. *Mexico.* New York: Thames and Hudson, 1984.

Collier, George, Renato Rosaldo, and John Wirth, eds. *The Inca and the Aztec State 1400–1800: Anthropology and History.* New York and London: Academic Press, 1982.

Cortés, Hernando. *Hernando Cortés: Five Letters 1519–1526.* Translated by J. Bayard Morris. New York: W. W. Norton, 1969.

Davies, Nigel, *The Aztecs.* New York: Putnam, 1974.

Díaz, Bernal del Castillo. *The Conquest of New Spain.* Translated by J. M. Cohen. Baltimore: Penguin, 1963.

Durán, Fray Diego. *The Aztecs: The History of the Indies of New Spain.* Translated by Doris Heyden and Fernando Horcasitas. New York: Orion Press, 1964.

_____. *Book of the Gods and Rites and the Ancient Calendar.* Translated and edited by Fernando Horcasitas and Doris Heyden. Norman: University of Oklahoma Press, 1971.

Fagan, Brian M. *The Aztecs.* New York: W. H. Freeman and Company, 1984.

Fuentes, Patricia de. ed. and trans. *The Conquistadors.* New York: Orion Press, 1963.

Gomara, Francisco Lopez de. *Cortés: The Life of the Conqueror by His Secretary.* Translated and edited by L. B. Simpson. Berkeley and Los Angeles: University of California Press, 1964.

Hassig, Ross. *Trade, Tribute, and Transportation: The Sixteenth Century Political Economy of Mexico.* Norman: University of Oklahoma Press, 1985.

_____. *Aztec Warfare: Imperial Expansion and Political Control.* Norman: University of Oklahoma Press, 1988.

León-Portilla, Miguel. *Aztec Thought and Culture: A Study of the Ancient Nahuatl Mind.* Translated by Jack Emory Davis. Norman: University of Oklahoma Press, 1963.

_____. *Pre-Columbian Literatures of Mexico.* Translated by Grace Lobanov and the author. Norman: University of Oklahoma Press, 1969.

_____. *The Broken Spears.* English translation by Lysander Kemp. Boston: Beacon Press, 1962.

McDowell, Bart. "The Aztecs." *National Geographic* 158, no. 6 (December 1980): 704-751.

Matos, Eduardo Moctezuma. *The Great Temple of the Aztecs: Treasures of Tenochtitlan.* Translated by Doris Heyden. London: Thames and Hudson, 1988.

_____. *Treasures of the Great Temple.* La Jolla: Alti Publishers, 1990.

Nicholson, Henry B. "Religion in Prehispanic Central Mexico." In *Handbook of Middle American Indians* Vol. 10, Part 1. Edited by G. Ekholm and I. Bernal. Austin: University of Texas Press, 1971.

Pasztory, Esther. *Aztec Art.* New York: Harry N. Abrams, Inc., 1983.

Robertson, Donald. *Mexican Manuscript Painting of the Early Colonial Period: The Metropolitan Schools.* New Haven: Yale University Press, 1959.

Sahagún, Fray Bernardino de. *Florentine Codex: General History of the Things of New Spain.* Translated by Arthur J. Anderson and Charles E. Dibble. Santa Fe and Salt Lake City: The School of American Research and The University of Utah, 1950–1982.

Sanders, William, Jeffery Parsons, and Robert Santley, eds. *The Basin of Mexico: Ecological Processes in the Evolution of a Civilization.* New York and London: Academic Press, 1979.

Soustelle, Jacques. *The Daily Life of the Aztecs on the Eve of the Spanish Conquest.* Translated by Patrick O'Brian. Harmondsworth: Penguin Books, Ltd., 1961.

Townsend, Richard. *State and Cosmos in the Art of Tenochtitlan.* Washington D.C.: Dumbarton Oaks, 1979.

Wolf, Eric. *Sons of the Shaking Earth.* Chicago: University of Chicago Press, 1959.

INDEX

maguey, 42
maize, 14, 17, 24, 50, 56
mayeque, 9
Mesoamerica, vii, 2, 3, 7, 38, 41, 48, 56, 65, 69, 70, 74
metlatl, 15, 23
Mictlan, 25
Mictlantecuhtli, 54
Mixcoatl, 39
Mixteca, 74
Mixtecs, 65
Moctezuma Xocoyotzin, vii, viii, 1, 2, 8, 28, 30, 32, 34, 39, 45, 47, 66, 76, 77, 78, 79, 80
Moctezuma, Eduardo Matos, vii, 63

Nahuatl, 2, 28, 40
National Institute of Anthropology & History, 59, 64
New Fire Ceremony, 44, 45
Nezahualpilli, 32
nobility, vii, 7, 8, 9, 13, 17, 20, 23, 27, 28, 30, 32, 33, 34, 38, 42
nobles, 8, 9, 12, 23, 25, 28, 30, 31, 33, 35, 39, 41, 50, 71
nopal cactus, 5

olla, 14
Olmec, 7, 38, 70

patolli, 39
pipiltin, 9
Pleiades, 45
pochtecah, 9, 27, 28
Precolumbian, 2, 3, 16, 57
Prehispanic, 3, 14, 65
priest, 2, 3, 7, 8, 9, 18, 31, 33, 40, 42, 43, 45, 52
Puebla, 74
pulque, 25
pyramid, 3, 7, 8, 11, 41, 47, 58, 63

quachtlacalhuaztli, 21
Quecholli, 39
quechquemitl, 21
quetzal, 25, 40
Quetzalcoatl, 7, 20, 26, 31, 32, 56, 57, 77, 78

ritual, 14, 15, 17, 22, 23, 28, 35, 37, 38, 40, 41, 42, 43, 44, 47, 48, 50, 52, 53, 65, 70, 71
Rodríguez, María de la Luz, 65

sacred precinct, 7, 8, 35, 58, 66
sacrifice, 4, 24, 25, 28, 31, 37, 41, 42, 44, 45, 47, 50, 51, 52, 53, 58, 63, 65, 73
Sahagún, Bernardino de, 2, 21, 30, 39, 60
Seven Caves, 4
soothsayers, 8, 24
stucco, 11, 35, 38, 68

Aztec warrior (from the Codex Mendoza*).*

tamales, 14, 15, 24, 34
Tamoanchan, 4
Tarascan, 6, 51
techcatl, 58
tecuitlatl, 16
telpochcalli, 23
Templo Mayor, 2, 7, 8, 35, 42, 45, 47, 58, 59, 60, 63, 66, 67, 68, 69, 70, 73, 74, 75

Tenochtitlan, 1, 2, 3, 5, 6, 7, 8, 10, 11, 14, 18, 26, 27, 28, 30, 32, 35, 37, 38, 41, 43, 45, 47, 48, 57, 58, 59, 66, 70, 74, 76, 77, 78, 80, 81, 82
Teoculhuacan, 3
Teotihuacan, 3, 7, 44, 67, 70, 75
tetecutin, 9
Tezcatlipoca, 1, 31, 46, 47, 57
ticitl, 21
Tlacatzinacantli, 65
tlachtli, 38
Tlacopan, 6
tlacotin, 9
tlacuilo, vii
Tlahuicole, 51
Tlaloc, 7, 16, 17, 25, 49, 50, 58, 68, 70, 71, 72, 73, 75
Tlalocan, 25
tlameme, 28
Tlatelolco, 2, 26, 27, 58, 82
tlatoani, 30
tlatoque, 9
Tlaxcalla, 6, 77, 80
Tlaxcalteca, 51
Tochancalqui, 62
Tocuepotzin, 33
Toltec, vii, 6, 7, 20, 31, 32, 40, 56
toltecah, 9, 20
Tonacatecuhtli, 25
Tonacatepetl, 56, 58
tortillas, 14, 15
Triple Alliance, 6, 7, 9, 30
Tula, 31
Tzapotlatena, 21
Tzompantitlan, 62

Valley of Mexico, vii, 3, 4, 6, 7, 8, 11, 12, 17, 19, 31, 41, 45, 67, 77
Veracruz, 76

Xipe Totec, 51, 57, 64, 65
Xiuhcoatl, 62
Xiuhtecuhtli, 42, 48, 49
Xochimilco, 13
Xolotl, 57

Yucatan Peninsula, 28, 76

Zapotecs, 65
Zócalo, 59